The Only Child

Myths and Reality

Ann Laybourn
Centre for the Study of the Child and Society
University of Glasgow

EDINBURGH: HMSO

*To my parents, for my childhood,
and to my daughters, for theirs*

© Crown copyright 1994
First published 1994

Applications for reproduction should be made to HMSO Bristol Library
Cataloguing in Publication Data.
A catalogue record for this book is available from the British Library

ISBN 0 11 495124 1

Contents

Preface

Only children seem to be making something of a comeback. For years the one-child family has been the least popular of family sizes, as most couples with any pretensions to parenthood felt obliged to make a proper job of it by having at least two. Over the past ten or fifteen years, however, while we in the West have been exclaiming over the consequences of China's "One Child" policy, a quieter revolution has been taking place nearer home. In many different countries, for many different reasons, more and more couples are having just one child.

But many parents of only children worry about how their child will turn out, and other couples who would like to stop at one are anxious about the after-effects. Is it fair to children to deprive them of brothers and sisters? Does it hamper their development and make it harder for them to get on with other people and to become independent of their parents? Are only children as happy and well-adjusted as other children? What about the effects in later life – how do adult only children cope with looking after elderly parents, and do they come to regret not having grown up in a larger family? Is it easier for children to cope with circumstances such as divorce or separation if they have brothers and sisters to support them?

This book, which is based on extensive research and interviews with one-child families, sets out to answer these and many other questions.

- The book does not try to persuade anyone to have an only child.

- It does set out the facts, so that parents and prospective parents can decide for themselves whether it is the right thing for them.

- It does not give a recipe for bringing up an only child.

- It does suggest some of the possible ingredients that may go towards a happy and successful only childhood, so that parents can combine them to suit their own circumstances.

- It does not claim that the one-child family is the perfect place for a child.

- It does argue that it is as good as any other.

- If you are the parent of an only child, or thinking of becoming one ...

- If you are an only child yourself, or married to one ...

- If you deal with children and families as part of your job ...

- If you are simply interested in what difference growing up without brothers and sisters makes to a child ...

this book was written for you.

Acknowledgements

Many people have contributed to this book. I should particularly like to thank Malcolm Hill and Stewart Asquith of the Centre for the Study of the Child and Society, and Rex Taylor of the Department of Social Policy for their help and encouragement; my colleague, Jane Brown for help in developing and clarifying my ideas; the ESRC Data Archive for providing the National Child Development Study dataset; Mary Latham for carrying out the computer analysis; Tom Aitchison for statistical advice; Janie Fergusson for computer searches of the literature on only children; Margaret Lamb for researching biographies; Beryl Riley for an early look at her thesis; Laura Lochhead for typing the manuscript; and my friend, Penny Roberts, for her lovely drawings of only children with their families and friends.

Very special thanks are due to all the families who so generously shared their experiences and views with me, and to my husband, who supported me financially and in many other ways while I was researching and writing the book.

Myths and Reality

"If it ain't broke, don't fix it." (Bert Lance)

The Myth

The scene is a local radio show for children in a park in one of Britain's major cities. The date is 1990. Children are queuing up to take part in a light-hearted talent contest. Up on stage comes a seven-year-old girl. The compere asks her name, where she lives, where she goes to school. Then:

"Have you got any brothers?"
"No."
"Any sisters?"
"No."
"Oh, you're an *only* child!" (One jocular eye on the audience,) "Are you lonely? Are you spoiled?"

This real-life event witnessed by a colleague of mine is not an isolated incident. Ask anyone what they think of only children, and unless they are one or have one themselves, the chances are high that you will get a reply along the lines of "spoiled, lonely and maladjusted". Ask what they think of parents who have an only child and the answers will range from "unfortunate", if the parents have one child through circumstance, to "selfish", if it is through choice. This stereotype seems deeply ingrained in the British consciousness, and surfaces periodically in fiction, in the media and even in educated conversation in a way that would now be unthinkable if the references were to ethnic minorities or to women. (Substitute "black", "delinquent" and "thick" for "only", "lonely" and "spoiled" in the anecdote above, and imagine the resulting furore.)

Even parents of only children seem to agree that they are missing out on something important, and that their child may suffer as a result. As one mother said sadly, "To me, one is not a family at all." And another interviewed for a national paper agrees.

My idea of a family is to have more than one child ... my family definitely feels incomplete. ... Even though we are constantly viewing and reviewing [his] behaviour and try very hard not to spoil him, the fact remains that because we have no other children we give him more attention than is good for him. (*Independent,* 8 February 1993)

And many only children themselves confirm the picture, as a selection of biographies and autobiographies picked very much at random from public library shelves shows. Gordon Kaye says

Both my parents loved me, of that I was always sure ... But I suppose being somewhat over-protected .... and being given quite overpowering affection, particularly from my mother, made me very self-conscious ... I was awkward, shy, dreadfully inhibited.

John Cleese sums up his upbringing in one word: "Sheltered". He describes his family as a tight, rather lonely, extremely loving but inward-looking little unit, driven by his father's hard work and his mother's smothering neuroticism. He was regarded as "delicate" and never allowed a bike. Even in his late teens his parents overcherished him. As a result, he felt he grew up socially awkward, unable to cope with the rough and tumble of school life.

I had a lot of problems about asserting a normal healthy aggression. I think that went on for a long time; even at Clifton [school] when I was playing soccer, I didn't like the violent side of it, and if someone kicked me, almost on a point of principle I wouldn't kick them back. It's taken me many years to get any confidence in that sort of self-assertive behaviour.

Roy Plomley gives a similar picture of a solitary childhood protected by his parents and with few playmates.

As I believe is common with an only child, I invented a companion. His name was Harry and he went with me everywhere. I would not go for a walk unless Harry was coming; I would not eat up my food until I was assured that Harry had eaten his ... Harry was a great comfort to me and I am sure he fulfilled a need.

In his "virtual solitude" he read voraciously, though second-hand and public-library books were not allowed in the house for fear of infection. He enjoyed films about college life because "The characters went about in a high-spirited gang, and I longed to be part of a gang".

Rita Hunter (opera soprano) describes a working-class childhood as a sickly child in the centre of a large extended family of adults – she had a thyroid deficiency and was therefore overweight. She had no real friends of her own age.

> I was never allowed in the street to play with other children except in the heat of summer and then I would only stand on our doorstep, being refused admission to a game of rounders. "She's too fat to run, we don't want her." I was much happier playing the piano or helping Dad to mend the punctures on his bicycle.

Bob Boothby describes himself as doted on by his well-to-do parents – home was "like living in a lukewarm bath". He was spoilt, excessively admired and his life was very precocious. Boarding school at the age of ten came as a shock. He was lonely and miserable and had no friends apart from the headmaster and his wife and the music teacher.

> When a boy has more in common with his teacher than his contemporaries, this is a clear sign of precocity and the result of being brought up as an only child in a home of adults, who treat him like an adult and who enjoys the experience.

The public at large, one-child parents and even only children themselves seem united in the belief that the one-child family is less than desirable. And that attitude has in the past deterred many parents from stopping at one.

The Changing Fortunes of the One-child Family

Over the past hundred years the popularity of the one-child family has waxed and waned. Until the late 19th century, a family with an only child must have been a rarity. Most people had large families, partly because that was what came along, partly because, in farming communities in which most people lived, many hands made lighter work. Only children were mostly the result of misfortune – when one or both parents died, or when, having produced one child, the mother was unable to have another.

However, between the First and Second World Wars, only children became fashionable. People were moving away from the farms to the cities, where children meant expense, not profit. Contraception and abortion had become more widely available, and parents had begun thinking in terms of "quality" of children rather than quantity. The recession and the atmosphere of insecurity it created provided another incentive for parents to keep their families small. According to a Royal Commission Report, a quarter of all couples who married in 1925 ended up with only one child.

After the Second World War, there was a new optimism, coupled with better economic prospects. Suddenly, larger families were all the rage again, and in the "Baby Boom" years to have only one child was very much seen as second best. However, in the 1970s and 80s family sizes became smaller again, and you might have expected a renewed interest in the one-child family. In fact the opposite is true. Population figures show that its popularity continued to decline, as more and more parents opted for two or three children, avoiding both large families of four or more, and the one-child family. Of women born in 1920, who on average had their first child around 1945, 21 per cent had one child. For those born in 1945, who had their first child around 1970, the figure is down to 13 per cent.

That pattern may seem surprising, but the reason for it is clear. Research studies from the 1970s suggest that one of the main reasons why parents chose to have a minimum of two was the deeply held belief that without brothers and sisters children grow up lonely and spoiled, and that it is therefore selfish to have only one. In 1980 a European Community (EC) survey revealed that a mere 2 per cent of British adults thought one child the ideal number.

However, there are indications that the pattern is changing. The same EC survey repeated in 1990, found that the popularity of the one-child family had increased fivefold, with 10 per cent of adults now considering it the ideal. Since in the past more couples have actually had an only child than considered it ideal, it seems likely that the survey reflects a real upturn in the fortunes of the one-child family in Britain.

It would be nice to be able to confirm that with some hard facts about the proportion of couples who now have an only child. Unfortunately, it is impossible. The reason is that you can never be certain how many children a woman is going to have until she reaches the menopause. By that time she will be twenty years away from the age at which most women have their first child. So "completed family size" as it is called, though the only reliable indicator, is always a couple of decades out of date. We know what proportion of women had only children in the 1970s, but not now.

For that we have to turn to measures that are up to date, but less reliable. Census returns are not a good guide. They give the proportion of parents who have one dependent child, but that merely tells you how many households happen to contain one child at any point in time. Every family (unless they have twins) starts off by having one child, and (unless the children all leave home at once) ends up that way too. Many of these one-child households are multi-child families in disguise. So census returns get us no further.

There is a better way of trying to find out what family size couples are tending to opt for, and that is to ask women of childbearing age how many children they expect to have. But this method has the opposite faults to "completed family size" – it is up to date but unreliable. Because having an only child is considered rather odd, fewer women give "one" as the answer than actually end up having one. So "expected family size" underestimates the proportion of one-child families that will actually be formed. If we bear this in mind, it is interesting that in 1986 the proportion of women in their late thirties and early forties who expected to have only one child was 10 per cent, whereas in 1991 it was 13 per cent. It's a modest rise, but taken together with the EC survey results, and the fact that average family size is now down to 1.8 children per family, it suggests that one-child families are on the increase.

If that is so, we are finally catching up with what is already happening in other Western countries. Taking average family size figures together with "ideal family size" views, it is clear that the one-child family is already a popular option in much of the European Community (as it is in the USA). To many people's surprise, such child-worshipping Mediterranean countries as Spain, Portugal, Italy and Greece have taken to the one-child family with enthusiasm – the EC survey shows that around 20 per cent of adults in Spain and Portugal believe one child is the ideal number.

In these countries the one-child family has been hailed as a new lifestyle for the 21st century. With women increasingly working outside rather than inside the home, having only one child makes it easier to combine the desire for parenthood with the desire for a career. With world population set to go through the roof it makes sense to limit to a minimum the number of children you bring into the world for your own enjoyment. And in times of economic pressure, one child costs less. Increasing numbers of one-parent families also mean more only children, as partnerships split up before another child arrives.

So for a number of reasons, we can probably expect more one-child families in the Britain of the future, and there are already indications that attitudes to only children are softening as we head for the 21st century. A study of newspaper references to only children in the late 1980s shows the stereotype in full swing. In contrast, over the past three years there has been much more balanced coverage of the subject in quality papers, women's magazines, radio and television. But it is clear that many of the old myths still persist, and that parents are still anxious about them. A recent letter seeking advice reads:

> I have a son aged four. I would love to provide him with a brother or sister but my husband says it is out of the question for financial reasons and that we cannot have more children. I am terribly worried about my son growing up as an only child and find myself in constant conflict with my husband. I have even considered divorce because I feel so strongly about this. What should I do? (*Observer Magazine*, 4 April 1993)

Some men feel the same way. A thirty-year-old lawyer whose wife had left him with a three-year-old boy challenges the belief that growing up without a mother is damaging to a child by saying

> I think it's more detrimental to Stuart being an only child than coming from a broken home. I always wanted to have lots of children and this is one of my major disappointments. (*Scotland on Sunday*, 4 November 1993)

And little wonder that parents are still concerned about the myths, when a recent edition of the *Independent* devoted a full-page spread to reinforcing them in a feature entitled "Does Only Have to Mean Lonely?" (8 February 1993). Almost the whole page is taken up with interviews with two only children and two one-child parents. The bold headlines run "I'm no breeding machine", "An incomplete family", "I detested children's parties" and "Three is a bad number". Three of the four interviews give an almost entirely negative picture of the one-child family. Only if you look carefully will you find, tucked away in the left hand corner, above an advertisement for light adapters, one column inch that refers to the positive findings of research.

Nor will parents have been much reassured by a recently published book by two only children, Jill Pitkeathly and David Emerson, entitled "*Only Child – How to Survive Being One*". The book is based on interviews with over sixty adult only children, many of whom seem to have had personal and relationship problems. The interviews and the authors' comments portray the only child as essentially different from other people. They claim that growing up without siblings leaves children with a "legacy of burdens", which become more troublesome as they get older; hindering close relationships, creating difficulties at work and producing a sense of permanent isolation. Some only children may appear confident and socially poised, they say, but underneath this polished exterior lies guilt-ridden turmoil. Only children are emotionally immature – unable to share, to stand up for themselves, or to take criticism and teasing. Many have particular difficulties in adapting to marriage, in making friendships, and in coping with special occasions such as Christmas. All the only children interviewed "expressed strong negative feelings about some or all of the experience" and "for the most part they echo the words of the only child who said 'There hasn't been a day in my life when I haven't wished for a brother or a sister.'" Their main message to parents planning to have one child is "Don't!"

Although from time to time the authors briefly state that being an only child can have some positive spin-offs (but some people said the same of being in Belsen, remarks one interviewee), the book basically presents lack of siblings as deeply damaging. It contains a "survival guide" to help adult only children and their partners cope and make the best of the situation. The authors say that writing the book has helped them to come to terms with their own experiences. "Don't think you can ignore your only-child background" they warn. "It is what has shaped you. You can learn to live with the effects, but you can't ignore them."

What should we make of this book? Well, it certainly shows that some only children have unhappy experiences. But how typical are those sixty bitterly regretful adults? Other books based on interviews with adult only children have come up with a much more balanced picture, which suggests that Pitkeathly and Emmerson may have lighted on a particularly problem-ridden group.

The book also shows that some adult only children believe their personal problems stem from the fact that they lacked brothers and sisters. But how realistic are they being? Sibling children have been known to have the odd problem too, so are only children really so different? Do they in fact turn out less happy and well-adjusted than other people? Does growing up without siblings really hamper emotional development and social skills?

These questions cannot be answered by canvassing the subjective opinions of a particular group of only children, any more than you can establish the therapeutic efficacy of a drug simply by asking people whether they feel it is doing them good. To find out the effect of a drug you have to carry out an objective comparison between the health of patients who take it and those who don't. And to find out whether having brothers and sisters is essential to normal development you have to compare the social and emotional health of only children and children with siblings. Research which does that comes up with a very different picture.

The Reality: What this Book is About

What does research tell us? What are one-child families really like? Are only children the fat, lonely, shy, inhibited, overprotected, self-centred, socially inept bunch they are made out and make themselves out to be? Are one-child parents selfish individuals, depriving their child of a normal, happy life in order to pursue their own interests?

When I first became interested in the subject of only children, I had no idea what the answers to those questions were. My own experiences led me to suppose that while some only children had problems, others did not. My idea was to write a book for parents and prospective parents, pointing out the pitfalls, and giving helpful advice on how to avoid them. As an essential first step I started to look at the research that had already been done on only children. It was an eye-opener. The more I read, the lower my jaw dropped, and the stronger became my conviction that what parents of only children primarily needed was not advice, but information. They needed to know the reality behind the myths.

For there is, in fact, a great deal of research on only children, and almost all of it is reassuring. The trouble is that most of it is out of sight. It is buried in academic books and journals, conference proceedings and PhD theses, most only available through specialist libraries. Some of it is couched in language (and figures) that are baffling even to a regular *Guardian* reader. Much of it is heavy going. It is uneven in quality, so that it is possible to stumble on one particular study and be totally misled – the evidence has to be looked at as a whole.

This book takes a long hard look in the light of research evidence at the claims that are made about only children and their parents. In it I have tried to present the evidence in a readable and user-friendly way. I have not assumed that the reader has any prior knowledge of social science, statistics and research methods, and where such things are essential to understanding the evidence I have tried to explain them as simply as possible. But I have not glossed over the difficulties. The reality of what only children are like is complex, as are the reasons behind the myths that surround them, and it is doing them a disservice to pretend otherwise.

Most of the research on only children comes from the USA, where, over the past twenty years, government funding has been generous in sponsoring studies on various aspects of one-child families. The one problem is that it might not necessarily apply to only children in Britain. From previous research I had done, I knew that British only children came from rather different social backgrounds from those in the USA. That could affect how they turned out. There has been no other published British research that relates specifically to only children. To check out whether US research held true across the Atlantic, I turned to one of the biggest studies of children ever undertaken.

The National Child Development Study (NCDS) is a long-term research project which has been following up every child in England, Scotland and Wales born between the 3rd and 9th of March 1958. So far there have been five follow-up "sweeps" – in 1965 when they were aged 7, in 1969 when they were 11, in 1974 when they were 16, in 1981 when they were 23, and in 1991 when they were 33. In the first three sweeps, information about their family circumstances and their physical, social and educational development was collected from parents, teachers and doctors, and from the youngsters themselves. In the last two sweeps, the adults have supplied information about their work, leisure, health, families, and ideas about life. In the most recent follow-up, their partners and their children have also given information.

A long-term study like the NCDS is a goldmine to researchers. Since it picked up every child in Great Britain born in one week, and since there is no reason to suppose there was anything peculiar about that week, we can be confident that what applies to those individuals as they grew up will apply to all other British children born around that time. The children are what is known as a "representative" sample. So we can generalise from the results of the study to other children, provided we remember that they may not apply to those born much earlier or much later than 1958.

The NCDS has been the basis for many influential publications produced by the original researchers. Some of these have looked at the effect of family size on child development, but only children have usually been lumped together with those from two-child families, which makes it impossible to tell how they fare by themselves. However, thanks to modern statistical computing it is possible for other researchers who have a particular interest they want to follow up to get relevant information from the original surveys and carry out their own "secondary analysis" of it. With the help of a colleague who is a computer programmer I decided to use it to look at how only children in the NCDS compared with children who had brothers and sisters – what backgrounds they came from, and how they turned out as they grew up. Our analysis was a comparatively modest exercise, aimed at checking out whether US findings applied to children in Britain, and the results are given here very briefly and simply. More detailed, complex and "academic" results will be published elsewhere. Information from the 1991 sweep became available just as this book was nearing completion, and we have included a few preliminary findings here; others will be published in due course.

One problem with studies which follow children over a long period of time is that many of them drop out – they decide they no longer want to take part, or move and cannot be traced, or they may simply miss one of the sweeps. So the numbers get smaller as the study progresses. That is not necessarily a problem as long as the groups you are comparing are losing the same kind of families at roughly the same rate. Luckily, the two main groups I wanted to compare, one-child and two-child families, had both lost comparatively few children over the years.

The first thing we had to do was to decide which of the NCDS children would count as only children and which as children with siblings. That was harder than it looks. Some children who have no brothers and sisters grow up with other children in the house (if, for example, their parent remarries and they acquire step-siblings). Some children who do have brothers and sisters effectively grow up on their own (as my two daughters have done, separated by an eighteen year age gap). Complications like these could make it look as if only children and sibling children were more like each other than they really are. Since the point of our analysis was to try to find differences between only and sibling children, it was important to eliminate factors which could mask them.

For that reason, all the "only children" in our analysis are children whose mothers had only one birth, who have no brothers and sisters, and who were the only child in the household at 7, 11 and 16. All the children from two-child families are those whose mothers only had two births, who have only one brother or sister, and who were one of two children in the household at 7 and 11. (By 16 many second children's older siblings would have left home although they had been around for the rest of their lives, and I did not want to exclude them.) We took similar steps to pick out children from three-, four- and five-child families. To avoid further complications, we excluded all multiple births and also left out children who had been adopted or who were in care. However, we included both one- and two-parent families.

The result is that our comparison is between only children, and children who come from fairly closely spaced families of between two and five. All the children will have been with their parent or parents since birth, and none will have had siblings who died or were stillborn. They are, therefore, children who have had fairly "normal" circumstances, according to current notions. Few families now have more than five children, and most try to space them closely.

Having done that, we were left with 416 only children, 2010 children from two-child families, and 4042 children from families of between three and five children – a total of 6468 children. These numbers are comfortably large enough for statistical analysis. So the results you find in this book should be reliable in confirming or challenging US findings.

However, a book based entirely on statistical information makes uninspired reading. To echo Alice in Wonderland's complaint, it has "no pictures or conversations". However reliable, statistics cannot bring to life the reality and variety of what it is like to be or to have an only child. To remedy that defect, I asked 20 only children and parents of only children to talk to me in depth about their experiences and ideas. Some were already known to me, others were found for me by colleagues and friends. They were chosen to give as wide a range of ages and social backgrounds as possible – in most cases I had no idea when I went to see them how they felt about their situation. The youngest only child I talked to was 11, the oldest 70, and their parents ranged from professional couples to unskilled labourers. Unless otherwise identified, all the quotations in the book come from taped interviews with those families, with names changed to preserve confidentiality. The interviews were not entirely one-sided: I talked about my experiences too, and a few of the minor quotes are mine, again disguised.

You will see from this as from the rest of the book that I give more weight to some research findings than to others. That is because some studies are more reliable than others. In general, the larger and more representative a study is, and the more factors it takes into account, the more we can assume that its findings will apply to similar groups of people. Very small studies (like the twenty families I talked to) can be useful in suggesting ideas and illuminating our understanding, but they can be misleading and have to be treated with caution (those twenty people I talked to might have been untypical of only children and their parents).

There is safety in numbers from another point of view, too. If a series of large-scale studies based on different groups from different countries all come up with much the same findings, we can be confident of their results. If there are only one or two studies on a topic and they point in different directions, we have to weigh up which is the most reliable and therefore most likely to be right. Because of that, where studies (including my analysis) confirm each other, I have described them fairly briefly. Where they contradict each other, I have gone into more details so that you can judge their reliability for yourself. In every case, I have given the reference for the study either in the text or in the Notes at the back of the book, so that you can check them out if you want to. A brief summary of results from our NCDS analysis is given in the Appendix.

Names

What should you call children who have brothers and sisters? Reluctantly, after writing it out time after time, I have abandoned "children who have brothers and sisters" in favour of "sibling children" or, in the case of a child from a two-child family, "one-sibling child". "Sibling" sounds a bit formal, but it is simple and in common use, as in "sibling rivalry".

What should you call children who have no brothers and sisters? Many people dislike the term "only child" because of its negative connotations, and they have come up with a variety of alternatives, all of which have disadvantages. "A child from a one-child family" is technically correct and emotionally neutral, but it is cumbersome, and I have discovered to my cost that people misread or mishear it and assume you are talking about children from one-*parent* families. "Single child" is quite popular, but ambiguous; it can also mean an adult child who is unmarried. "Singleton" is sometimes used in academic texts, but it is rather formal. In the USA only children are often referred to as "onlies" or "solos", but I cannot bring myself to use either.

In the end I have decided to stick with "only child". It is easy to use and has the great virtue of being immediately understood by almost everybody. As for its connotations, we should know by now that simply changing the label does not help. The point is to change perceptions. My own experience as an only child was a happy one, and I have enjoyed having two "only" children. To me "only child" rings positive. I hope by the end of this book it will to you too.

Finally, all authors of books about children are faced with the tricky question of what sex they are. In less gender-conscious days they all just wrote "he" and "him", and everyone understood that applied to girls as well as boys. However, many people now find that off-putting, and authors have resorted to a variety of other devices: always referring to "he/she", or using "he" and "she" in alternate chapters or even alternate paragraphs. I have taken an old-fashioned approach and used the pronoun "they" which is nicely non-committal and which, though frowned on by grammarians, has a respectable literary history of use with singular nouns where sex is uncertain. I hope no devotee of Fowler's *Modern English Usage* ends up tearing their (his/her) hair out.

CHAPTER ONE

Is it Selfish to have an Only Child?

"The only child is the product of a couple who consider, who calculate, who often have ambitions ... but who who have a horror of the unexpected, the uncertain, who have no faith in the future; in a word, who love their own lives, but who don't love Life!" (Colombusier)

The Claim

The rather extreme pronouncement from a French childcare expert quoted above appeared forty years ago, but echoes of it have rung on up to the present day. "When we had no children we were told that we were selfish. Now that we've got one we're still being told that we're selfish", says a father in the *Independent,* (8 February 1993). US studies of popular attitudes to one-child families have found that many people believe parents of only children to be rather self-centred, irresponsible people, only marginally committed to parenthood and refusing to have more than one child because of the inconvenience it could put them to. To put it bluntly, they are selfish.

Is popular opinion right?

The Reality

We start off with a major problem. We know far more about why parents do not have only children than about why they do. For all the theorising that has been done about one-child parents, there are very few research studies which have actually got down to asking them why they have chosen to defy convention in that way. So we are in a relatively unexplored area here and any conclusions we draw have to be quite tentative.

Let us start with the few facts we do have. We know something about what sort of parents only children are born to. In the USA they tend to be either older couples with higher-than-average levels of education and dual careers in high status jobs, or single parents, usually mothers, also more likely than average to have fulltime jobs.

In Britain, a fair proportion of only children also come from single-parent families, and their mothers, whether married or not, tend to be older than average and more likely to work fulltime. However, in contrast to the USA, British only children have not tended to come from families where parents are at the top of the educational and occupational ladder, but those about half-way up it, with fathers who had left school early and gone on to skilled working-class jobs. That was true for Scottish children born in 1969–70 and for British children in the National Child Development Study (NCDS) born in 1958. NCDS only children were also more likely to be living in accommodation without sole use of such basic amenities as a hot-water supply, a fixed bath and an indoor toilet.

Of course, only children in Britain come from all social levels. But it seems that, far from being born with a silver spoon in their mouths, as people suggest, many in fact have parents with only moderate levels of education and income, who are having something of a struggle to make ends meet. That suggests that parents may choose to have only one child in order to give that child as much as possible of the limited resources they have.

However, the trouble with this information is that it is out of date. It tells us about what sort of parents were having only children twenty or thirty years ago, not what they are doing now. In the 1990s more parents seem to be choosing to have an only child, but we have little idea why since no one has asked them.

On a global level, it seems clear that new employment opportunities for women have contributed to a rise in one-child families – the logistical problems of managing two careers are simplified if there is only one child to find substitute care for. People have suggested to me that we may have shifted over to the US pattern of one-child families – that British only children are now also likely to be the choice of highly educated, aspiring professional couples. That is possible – we just do not know. Certainly the rise in single-parent families will have led to a corresponding rise in only children as partnerships dissolve before more children arrive. The fact that more women are postponing their first birth into their late thirties and early forties will mean that some have no chance of (or too little energy for) a second birth. Economic factors have probably also played a part; it seems that one-child families become more popular in a recession (their numbers rose in the 1920s and 1930s and seem to have risen again in the past decade); one child creates less expense than two.

But we cannot go much further than that. When large-scale opinion polls ask people hypothetically why they might not have more than one child, they mention issues such as housing shortages, poor childcare provision, poor job prospects and so on, but that is obviously not the whole answer, since, faced with these very problems, many other people go on to have larger families. A US study found that "financial problems" was the chief reason parents gave for having an only child, but it was also the chief reason other parents gave for having two. Some researchers have suggested that people give these reasons because they are the easiest answer; they are socially acceptable rationalisations of decisions that are in fact much more complex.

One child through necessity

Of course, some parents do not decide to have an only child at all – they simply have one thrust upon them by fate. Mothers may develop medical conditions, such as asthma or angina, that make it inadvisable for them to risk another pregnancy. Or they may be left with one child when the other parent is lost to the family through death, divorce or separation. Some mothers find they are simply unable to conceive again or carry another child to term, as had happened in one family I interviewed.

> I had a miscarriage before Lucy, and I had another when she was three and a half and at that point, after that one, I couldn't watch pictures of baby animals on television without going into floods of tears, which was very difficult for her. I remember once there was something nice and sentimental on the television and I said "Oh" and she recognised the tone of voice and said "It's alright, Mummy, there's no baby" and I thought "Heavens, what am I doing to this child?" Somebody seems to have done a study on this "secondary infertility" and discovered it is at least as painful as primary infertility, possibly more so. All the other children in the NCT [National Childbirth Trust] group the same age have siblings. That in itself is difficult. I just about coped with a wave of second babies because most of them actually came along before I lost the other one. But the third babies were difficult and one or two started having a fourth one. I'm still with the group, but I feel kind of on the edge of it.

One woman I spoke to was left as the sole child of the family when her much loved elder sister died. Another was an only child because:

> I was adopted. They were in their late forties, and they were about twelve years married, childless. My mother had had a number of

pregnancies that ended in miscarriage and then a pregnancy where the baby was born and lived a few hours. So eventually they decided to go for adoption. So that's how I arrived. When I was young, I think I was about the age of five, my mother was ill a lot because she then wanted to try for another child and was very ill. She would be in the hospital for months and months and months at a time. Most of my childhood I spent with my grandmother.

Not all the circumstances which lead to having an only child are so traumatic – several only children or one-child parents I interviewed said that another baby had simply never come along, and that had been accepted quite philosophically. But it is important to realise that some of the situations that have led to parents having only one child are distressing or difficult to come to terms with, and may make it harder for them to give their child the happy uncomplicated upbringing they would wish to. That is a point to bear in mind when considering how only children turn out.

One child through choice

Some researchers who have studied how parents decide on their family size, believe that they keep a kind of "profit and loss account". There are rewards from having children (the excitement of the birth, the pride in the first step, the first word, the first day at school, the love and kisses). There are also costs (the sleepless nights, the endless bickering, the rows and tantrums, the difficulty of juggling job and childcare, the need to find a babysitter every time you go out). Consciously or unconsciously, parents decide on the family size that will bring them maximum rewards with minimum costs. One of the rewards they take into account is social approval for "doing the right thing". So, though it may seem that having only one child would maximise profit and minimise loss, social disapproval of the one-child family is so great that it outweighs its practical advantages so far as most parents are concerned. If this line of reasoning is correct, parents who stop at one must see very great gains in that course of action (or drawbacks in having more) to offset the disapproval they will almost certainly encounter. How do parents of only children draw up their balance sheet?

Two US studies suggest that parents who choose to have an only child do so for a variety of reasons: the desire to have more personal freedom, or time for their careers or their marriages; reluctance to go through the baby stage again; anxiety about finance; concern about world population growth; and the wish to do the best they can for their child financially. An Australian study also found that mothers who had chosen to have one child were more career-oriented and less likely to have enjoyed the baby stage than mothers who wanted a second birth.

These reasons were similar to those of parents I interviewed. Practical restrictions such as housing and finance were certainly sometimes a factor, but rarely enough on their own to decide things.

[Father:] There's two reasons. The first reason you could say is the size of our flat; it's a bit awkward. But the real reason is that Anne went through postnatal depression, and I'm as happy as Anne is with just Natasha. [Mother:] I don't feel as though I want to go through that again. You really can't say it's going to happen again, but it's not something that I want to chance.

Clearly the bad experience after the birth was the major factor with this couple, as it was for another mother who had originally thought of having two children.

....even to the extent that Nick built an extension to the house that we rent at the moment and we had actually planned to put on two small bedrooms for the two children. I suppose I had my mind made up for me in that I had puerperal psychosis, and so I was in a psychiatric hospital for eight weeks after I had Ian, and I would say I wasn't completely better until he was two. It's almost impossible to describe to someone who's not experienced it. It's sort of full-blown, psychotic mental illness. Hearing voices and so on. Also the drugs that they gave me to calm me down rendered me incapable of walking and writing and things. It is one in two thousand pregnancies, which is actually quite a lot, and there is a chance of that recurring with a subsequent pregnancy to term. So that's the main reason. Having said that, I'm not entirely convinced that I would have ever had a second child anyway.

For one couple, the fact that their first baby screamed constantly for the first three months had been the deciding factor, but other parents with much calmer babies still found the early months had got them down.

Originally I thought if we had two they would keep each other company, but I found the baby stage very difficult, I found the extreme dependency very difficult, and by the time it got to the point where I might have thought of getting pregnant again, she was one and she had started to talk and she was walking around and she was sleeping through the night and I thought I just couldn't go back. It was so nice that life had at last taken on some shape again, I couldn't bear the thought of going back to all that again and it was at that stage that I decided about it.

Another mother had gone back to work when her first child was three and then found life had moved on to the point of no return.

People do ask you, don't they, when you've had one, quite soon after, they keep saying: "When are you having your next one?" and I don't think I would have thought about it until she was about four, really, getting over the sleepless nights, and then when the time gets on you're doing something else, aren't you? I think it would have been very difficult to go back. I think I would have found that difficult, to stay at home for another three years without anything else.

Children are hard work, and some parents who enjoy one feel two would be too much, as this mother of a late baby explained:

I felt I didn't have the strength, the energy. No, I felt I couldn't have coped again with another.

Others valued the quieter, more civilised life that having an only child makes possible:

I look at people with two children and I think: 'Is it worth the hassle?' All this shouting in the supermarket – and the three of us will go in, we'll have a nice cup of coffee somewhere and some child will be screaming. It just seems a nightmare for some people.

Clearly parents see advantages to themselves in having only one child. But they also see advantages to the child, as one woman who came from a working-class family points out.

I've talked to my mother about why I am an only child and she has always given the same reason, which is that they felt that they could provide better for one child than they could for more than one. My mother did very well at school and would have dearly liked to have gone into further education and didn't get the chance, and her younger brother was sent for further education instead. So I think she always felt very strongly that she would like that for me, and that having another child would perhaps compromise their abilities to support me.

We saw earlier that skilled working-class families were more likely to have an only child and it seems likely that considerations such as these enter into their decisions. Where money is tight, but you want your child to go further than you, it may make sense to concentrate resources in one child rather than spread them more thinly over two or more.

The desire to concentrate limited resources on one child can apply to time and attention as much as money, as this mother of a five-year-old explained:

Parenting takes a lot out of us. We want to give him as much as we can. We want to give him the chance of doing anything he wants. We feel that another child, no matter how much you loved both children, they would be vying for attention and you wouldn't be able to do everything.

Love is supposed to be an unlimited resource, but some parents feel that with a second child they might not be able to give the level of emotional commitment that they gave to the first. The same mother continued:

I like Stuart now, he's just at that age when he's exploring things, it's an exciting time and we love him so much that we can't honestly imagine loving another child as much. And I know that happens because my cousin has two children and she has realised she never loved the second child. They loved their first child so much that the second could never come up to their expectations. I think if they had had a boy it would have been different, but it was another daughter. I can't imagine I would be quite like that but at the same time, people say, oh you always love your children, but it doesn't always work that way.

And the mother of a two-year-old, who had not finally decided whether to have another, agreed:

I've actually got to the stage where I would worry more about having another one and trying to keep him from feeling jealous, because I have seen it so often, I have seen constant displays of jealousy. I'm not talking about when they're two, I'm talking about when they're thirty two! I've got friends where the phrase "Number one son" comes very much to mind, and the second son is constantly striving to be as good. I don't think an only child really has that problem.

Both these mothers are only children themselves, and it is possible that parents who have not experienced sibling relationships at first hand do not appreciate that love can be shared and that the affection and fun of brothers' or sisters' company can more than compensate for less attention from your parents. Maybe some only children have a jaundiced view of sibling relationships. On the other hand, recent research shows that jealousy and preferential treatment by parents are very real problems for some siblings, so it may be that only children are being fairly realistic. What does seem to be the case is that having been an only child yourself can make you much more aware of any possible benefits of life without siblings.

One child through tradition

Some people believe that only children are more likely than others to have a large number of children – they have been unhappy themselves so, to compensate, they try to create the big happy family they have missed. That is not true; only children tend to opt for small families. But do they want only one?

An Australian study from the early 1970s suggests not. Women who were only children were the least likely to name the one-child family and the most likely to name the two-child family as the ideal family size. Fifty-nine per cent of the only children felt they had missed out from not having siblings, so perhaps it is not surprising that they did not want to impose a similar situation on another child. However, of the 12 per cent who said they had positively enjoyed being an only child, none thought that the one-child family was too small.

"Ideal family size" is not, as we have seen, a very reliable guide to how many children you end up with. Most people give "two children" as their answer, because in Western society that is the norm, but the proportion of families having just two children is much smaller. Very few people give "one child" as their answer, because in our society that is considered rather odd – but a much higher proportion actually end up with one. So are only children in practice more likely to have an only child themselves?

Some French census information suggests that they are, and our analysis of the NCDS confirms it. Mothers of children in the study who were themselves only children were slightly more likely than those with siblings to have an only child themselves. It seems that when it comes to the point, only children are more likely to have one child themselves, despite social pressures and the fact that their partner will probably want more than one. That may be partly due to inherited low fertility, but it seems likely to be due also to more positive attitudes.

It is not necessarily that only children deliberately choose to have one child because they consider it the best option, though some certainly do. My interviews suggested that it may also have a subtler, more indirect effect. What seemed to have happened in several cases was that when parents, for some reason, found having another baby a bit problematic, they were, because of their own positive experience, happy to leave it at that. The mother who had puerperal psychosis felt this had been a factor in her decision not to risk it again.

> I don't worry about him being an only child at all and I suppose that's because I'm one myself.

It seems that for reasons like these, "chains" of only children can occur where the pattern is repeated over several generations. I met two adult only children whose mothers had been only children and who had an only child themselves. Here is one of them.

> Well in my mother's case, my grandfather died when I think she was about 15 and he had had TB before that, so that might have been something to do with it. I think possibly my grandparents' relationship was not particularly wonderful, but they were strict Roman Catholics so they stuck together. So that's possibly the reason why my mother's an only child.
>
> My mother went back to her career when I was five. She didn't plan to have a big family. I don't think she even planned to have me. I was born about nine months after she married, so I was a sort of honeymoon baby. She went back to work when I was five, and that was that. She never appeared to question it. She thought, well, she'd never had any brothers or sisters and she never felt that she'd been deprived. My father came from a big family. He felt more

uncomfortable about the fact, but I don't think either of my parents are particularly keen on children. I mean, they love me, they love their grandchild, they're very kind to children, very kind to their nephews and nieces, but I wouldn't say they're the kind of people to gush over babies or find anything interesting about them.

My father had three sisters, and one died when he was young. They obviously love each other but they don't particularly like each other. The two sisters don't get on at all. As long as I've been around there's always been tension and rivalry and competition. It has caused an awful lot of problems in the family. So that probably helped to put me off having brothers and sisters, and, certainly, my mother and I talked about it and said thank goodness we don't have this problem!

There are lots of reasons why we have an only child. From my point of view, I don't see the point of having any more. I was happy being an only child. And from my husband's point of view, he didn't particularly see any positive advantage to having a sister. I think perhaps it's also something to do with the question of the population, and that one child is enough in a sense, per family. The resources in the world are limited. And neither of us are into babies. I love my son, and I really enjoy him, but prior to having him, I wouldn't say I was particularly maternal. I have never been broody since having him. I've never wanted another child.

One child through seeing it work

Even parents who are not themselves only children may be reassured that having an only child is a good idea, if they know other one-child families whose children have turned out well.

Greg was a superb baby, he did all the right things at all the right times, we could take him anywhere, we could do anything, he wasn't a problem, but within a year I knew I didn't want to have any more. And Don didn't want to have any more. So that was the decision made. But, having said that, a lot of it was influenced by the fact that we have friends who have only children, and we've seen those children from about the age of nine right up until some of them are in their mid-twenties, and they were great children. I can see Greg in those children because they were the same kind of parents as we are – they did the same things as us, the children were part of their lives, they did things, they explained things to them, they got on well with them. They all went through a sort of rocky period at some point which I expect will happen, but basically those were just really nice children. I thought well, if he turns out like that, we've not lost anything. I have never regretted the decision.

One child through getting it right first time

Parents who opt for an only child forfeit their chance to have "one of each" – "a boy for you, a girl for me" – a son to play football with Dad and follow on in the family business, a daughter to stay at home with Mum and produce the grandchildren. US researchers have suggested that parents are more likely to stop at one child if they get a boy the first time. They have found that when they picked samples of only children, boys or men outnumbered girls or women.

I had expected to find the same. But I got one of the greatest surprises of my research life when I saw the computer printout. In the NCDS, only girls outnumbered only boys. Just as interesting, when I looked at the printout for children who were the first of two, boys outnumbered girls. That was not just true of the children I had selected; it applied to a lesser extent to the whole sample of children who had been the only or first child in the household at age seven.

NCDS parents who wanted a small family seem to have been more likely to stop at one if they had a girl first time. If they had a boy first time, they were more likely to have gone on to try for another child. It looks very much as if the worldwide preference for boys simply did not apply in the Britain of the late 1950s, and that one reason for having an only child was that you got a girl first time.

Maybe it is not so surprising that parents should have been more likely to opt for only girls. In the past, there were strong economic and social reasons for preferring boys, as there are today in many societies – boys get better jobs, do not need dowries, carry on the family name, confer higher status on their parents. The traditional desire for a male child has been one of the main stumbling blocks of China's "One Child" policy – faced with an only girl, parents have sometimes even resorted to infanticide to give themselves a second chance at conceiving a boy. But in Britain by 1958, opportunities for women had opened out sufficiently for girls to be perceived as having equal prospects of success at school and at work. A girl could therefore satisfy her father's desire to see his child get ahead, while simultaneously fulfilling her mother's wish for a pretty little girl to dress up, a female companion in the house and a caring daughter to provide support in old age. Girls could straddle the gender gap in a way that, in the comparatively macho world of 1958, boys could not.

A US study confirms that even in the 1980s only girls may have found it easier to fit in with both parents' expectations than only boys. Mothers and fathers both felt reasonably happy about only girls playing with "boys' toys" and about the prospect of them entering "male occupations" such as being a truck driver or a professor of engineering. But while mothers of only boys were fairly happy for them to play with "girls' toys" and enter "female occupations" such as being a secretary or a professor of home economics, fathers were quite strongly opposed to both. It was seen as more acceptable to allow masculine qualities in a girl than feminine ones in a boy.

Fascinating as these results are, they may be past their sell-by date. Parents feel more uneasy about sex stereotyping their children than they did even in the early 1980s. It may be that the rise of the "New Man" who combines ambition with caring and tenderness, will now leave Western parents equally happy with an only boy or an only girl. We do not know.

What is Selfish?

So to return to our original question – are parents who have an only child "selfish"? Clearly the ones who have no choice in the matter are not (though "no choice" is a relative concept – some parents who are left with one child because of circumstances such as death of the other child, secondary infertility or heart problems will feel they do have a choice and make herculean efforts to exercise it by pressing for IVF, adopting an older child, or risking their well-being with another pregnancy). But what about parents who have chosen to stop at one? If you have yourself gone to a deal of trouble to have two or three you may indeed see their desire for peace and quiet, their longing for a good night's sleep, their need to get back to work and their general lack of broodiness as confirmation that there is something missing in them as parents (though if you are honest, you may recognise those as reasons why you decided to stop at two or three). Although they also see positive benefits to their child in being the only one, they are certainly putting their own interests if not first, at least somewhere in the equation. But is that selfish?

The Oxford English Dictionary definition of the word is "Devoted to or concerned with one's own advantage or welfare *to the exclusion of regard for others*. The phrase I have italicised reminds us that simply doing what you want is not selfish. Selfishness is doing what you want when it harms someone else. The charge that one-child parents are selfish derives much of its force from the assumption that lack of brothers and sisters is damaging to a child. Parents are sacrificing their child's best interests to their own needs. The profit is theirs; the loss is the child's. Whether that is true we shall see in the following five chapters.

Summing-up

Parents who have one child are sometimes accused of being selfish, of pursuing their own interests at the expense of their child's. In fact, parents have only children for a variety of very complex reasons. Some are unable to have any more, others are trying to give their child maximum opportunities in terms of financial provision, education, time and attention. Some have had bad experiences of childbirth or its aftermath, or have found the early months of babyhood difficult or tedious and do not want to repeat them. Others value the freedom to work or lead an adult life that having an only child facilitates. Some have chosen to limit their family to one because of population concerns. For some of them, which sex of child they have first may be crucial.

    Some of these reasons are certainly to do with benefits to the parents, but they can only be said to be selfish if the parents' decision to stop at one is damaging to the child. We look at that question next.

CHAPTER TWO

Are Only Children High Achievers?

"Children with no siblings can be spoilt prima donnas, but they are often high achievers." (Independent on Sunday, 26 January 1992)

The Claim

Whatever their other defects, it is generally conceded that only children are clever. A favourite opening gambit in any article on the subject is the "name game" – a list of famous only children from various walks of life.

> Albert Einstein, Indira Ghandi and Franklin D. Roosevelt were only children, as are Brooke Shields, Billy Joel, John Updike, Ted Koppl, Lauren Bacall, Burt Bacharach, football great Roger Staubach and astronaut Frank Boorman. The King himself, Elvis Presley, was an only, too. That should comfort the increasing number of women who are considering having an only child. (*Cosmopolitan*, November 1989)

If the latter part of this list seems a touch too transatlantic, it would be easy enough to think up a British list: John Cleese, Marti Caine, Alan Ayckbourn, Andrea Newman, Penelope Lively, Alec Guinness, Gordon Kaye, Roy Plomley, Chris Bonnington, Jean Rook, Brian Redhead, John Simpson, Kate Adie, Nigel Lawson, Arthur Scargill, Roy Jenkins, Neil Kinnock.

It is not entirely clear what the point of these lists is. They are reminiscent of similar lists of famous people who have overcome conditions like asthma and epilepsy, intended to show children and their parents that such conditions need not be disabling: "You too can overcome the handicap of being an only child." But if, as is more often the case, the intention is to suggest that only children tend to be exceptionally high achievers, the name game is misleading. Quite apart from the fact that such lists, if they are honest, will include Joseph Stalin as well as Indira Ghandi (there is more than one way of being a high achiever), they in fact prove nothing. Certainly some famous people are only children; many are not. John Cleese is an only child; Stephen

Fry is one of three. Penelope Lively and Alan Ayckbourn are only children; Margaret Drabble and A.S. Byatt are sisters. Franklin D. Roosevelt was effectively an only child, having a half-brother many years older than himself; Margaret Thatcher, contrary to all appearances, is not. And while we are considering political leaders, Stalin was, Hitler wasn't.

An alternative gambit is the "numbers game".

> Only children score better on IQ tests, reach higher levels of education and get more prestigious jobs than people with siblings.
> (*Time,* 13 May 1991)

The numbers game sounds more convincing, as well as having a nice scientific ring to it. But, as we shall see, in a much more subtle way it is equally misleading.

The Reality

So what is the reality? Do only children have more intellectual ability and become higher achievers than those with siblings? The answer is complicated, because the question of how only children turn out, though it seems quite straightforward, in fact conceals two quite different questions, which have different answers.

How do only children compare with sibling children?

To approach this question scientifically we would ideally want to compare all only children with all children who have siblings. That is clearly impossible, so we have to find a sample of only and sibling children who are representative of all children, and of whom therefore, we can confidently say that anything that applies to them is also likely to apply to all other children born around the same time. The NCDS is such a study. So let us look at all the only children in the study and see how they compare with all the other children who came from family sizes of two, three, four and five children. Do the only children have more intellectual ability and are they higher achievers?

The answer to this question is a resounding "Yes". Compared with other children from larger family sizes, only children had higher average scores on tests of ability (IQ tests) which they were given when they were 11. They also had higher scores on almost every measurement of achievement that we looked at. When they were 7, their teachers rated them as more creative and more aware of the world around them, and they also had higher scores on a reading test, though there was no difference between only children and sibling children on an arithmetic test. When they were 11 they did better on both reading and maths tests and their teachers rated their general knowledge as superior, though only children were no more likely than sibling children to be considered "outstanding" in any respect. At 16 they had even higher scores than sibling children on tests of maths and reading comprehension, were more eager to get A levels or Scottish Highers, were more likely to be planning to go on to higher education and had higher job aspirations. By 23, they were more likely to be in work or in further education and less likely to be unemployed or economically inactive. Those in work were also more likely to be in higher status occupations, particularly professional ones.

These findings mirror very closely those from other studies which have asked the same question. The researcher who has done most work on how only children turn out is Toni Falbo, Professor of Educational Psychology at the University of Texas. As well as carrying out research of her own, she has several times examined the enormous number of studies of only children carried out by other researchers, to get an overall picture of their conclusions. In 1988 she got together with Denise Polit, who also had a research interest in only children, to do what is known as a "quantitative review" of 74 studies on the intellectual achievement of only children. A quantitative review (sometimes called a "meta-analysis") is a way of combining the scores from many research studies by a mathematical formula, to come up with an overall result. Polit and Falbo found that, compared with sibling children, only children scored significantly better in all types of ability test, with a particular advantage on tests of verbal ability (including reading), and this was true for both boys and girls and for children from different social classes and nationalities.

Findings such as these are what the numbers game is based on. Compared with all other children with siblings, only children do seem to have higher levels of ability and achievement. That means if you met an only child in the street, the chances are above average that they would be a high achiever. But if at this point you are getting depressed (or, alternatively, seething) because you have more than one child or are yourself a sibling child, cheer up (or calm down). That is only the answer to the first question.

Does being an only child affect how you turn out?

This is the question you are asking if what you want to know is whether it will make a difference if you have one child rather than two. And the numbers game is not a good way of answering it, as we shall now see. For, of course, how you turn out depends not just on whether or not you have siblings, but on all sorts of other factors.

Family size

It may seem blindingly obvious to say that only children come from small families, but it is a very important point. We know from research on the subject that the smaller a child's family is, the higher their intellectual ability level and their achievements are likely to be. A debate about the reasons for this has been raging for many years and is still going on. Some researchers argue that it is due to the greater availability of parental time and attention to each child in small families – adult input is not "diluted" by large numbers of children who lower the family's intellectual tone. Others argue that it is simply a matter of small families being better off and hence providing better social, economic and educational opportunities for their children. Others claim that the relationship between ability level and family size is all an illusion – it just happens that bright, educationally oriented parents (whose children would anyway inherit their bright genes and benefit from their intelligence-promoting environment) tend to opt for small family sizes. But however they explain it, no one seriously challenges the fact that children from small families tend to come out better in studies of ability and achievement.

That means, of course, that comparing only children with all other children from a variety of family sizes is not a good guide as to whether having or not having a sibling makes a difference. Because children who come from large family sizes will make up a hefty proportion of the group with siblings and because (for whatever reason) those children will tend to come out less well on tests such as these, only children enter the comparison with an unfair advantage. Nor, of course, is it a good guide from a practical point of view. Most prospective parents do not lie awake in the small hours wondering whether to give their only child four brothers and sisters; the choice they are hesitating between is one child or two. From both these points of view a much more reliable guide to whether having a sibling makes a difference is to restrict the comparison to children in the smallest family sizes – to compare only children with children who have just one sibling. That way we avoid the answer being complicated by the effect of family size.

Here is the twist. Comparing only children with one-sibling children, the only children now come off no better on many of the items and, in some cases, slightly worse. They are still slightly ahead on tests of reading and reading comprehension at every age. However, there is now no difference between the two groups of children on awareness of the world, creativity and general knowledge as rated by teachers. Nor do the only children at 16 have higher aspirations for further education and employment. Nor are they more likely at 23 to be employed or to be in a higher status occupation. They now actually do marginally less well than one-sibling children on tests of ability at 11 and on maths tests at every age. Overall, the tables have turned.

The fact that the only children did less well on ability (intelligence) tests seems to imply that if you want your child to be of superior intelligence you should provide them with a brother or sister (but only one!). That indeed is the line taken by two research psychologists, Zajonc and Marcus. They are fascinated by the fact that the general rule: "the smaller the family size, the higher the intellectual ability of the children" does not seem to hold true for the smallest size of all. You would expect that only children, coming from the smallest family size, would score the highest on intelligence tests. But in many studies (as in ours) they do not. Puzzling. In one-child families, adult input is at its most concentrated, so on average only children should do best of all. Why don't they? Zajonc and Marcus noticed that in some studies youngest children (of whatever family size) also show a puzzling decline in ability and that led them to come up with an ingenious answer. What both only children and youngest children lack is a younger sibling. Zajonc and Marcus suggest that the experience of helping and teaching (in their term "tutoring") a younger sibling benefits the intellectual development of the older child.

This idea seems to solve the puzzle neatly, and it has been quite widely accepted. It has even been taken up by some childcare experts who suggest that parents of only children should arrange for them to spend some time with younger ones, in order to enhance their intelligence. There is just one snag: the "tutoring hypothesis" does not work.

First, experiments have cast doubt on the suggestion that tutoring enhances learning – it does not seem to have much effect. Second, Zajonc and Marcus's theory does not pass a crucial acid test. If it was true, then in two-child families the first child would always tend to be significantly more intelligent than the second, and that does not seem to be the case – studies suggest there is very little difference between the two. And finally, as many researchers on family size have pointed out, there is a much simpler and more obvious explanation of why only children on average do less well than one-sibling children. What handicaps them is not the lack of a younger sibling, but the lack of a father.

Family separation

We saw in Chapter 1 that only children were much more likely than other children to come from a lone-parent family; indeed many are only children specifically because of that. Some research studies suggest that children of lone parents (whether divorced, separated or never married) tend to do less well in terms of achievement. (Again, there is a big debate as to why this is so, and it has been suggested that the main reason is that lone parents are poorer, and that it is poverty, rather than lack of a father as such, that results in their children's lower achievements.) Since more only children than one-sibling children come from one-parent families, that could account for their lower performance. That is the explanation put forward by a number of researchers who have made a study of only children and ability. It certainly seems to fit the evidence from the NCDS. Throughout their childhoods, only children were twice as likely as one-sibling children to have had no regular father figure. So could this account for their slightly poorer performance in ability tests?

The answer seems to be "up to a point". To test whether the dip in performance was due to lone parenthood, we reran all the ability and achievement indicators, this time only looking at children who had had two parents (and the same two parents) throughout their childhood and whose family had therefore remained "intact". There were 363 only children and 1848 children with one sibling.

The results were interesting. Only children were still better readers at every stage, as they had been before the lone-parent children were dropped. However, that was still their sole significant advantage. There were no differences between the two groups on teachers' ratings, maths scores and ability test scores, aspirations, or employment status. So when only children had had a stable father figure throughout their childhood, they had only managed to draw level with the one-sibling children except in reading at which they still excelled.

Economic and social factors

There were of course a number of other aspects of only children's backgrounds which could have affected their performance. As we saw in Chapter 1, only children tend to come from rather different backgrounds from sibling children. Compared with children with one sibling, NCDS only children were less likely to have come from either very affluent or very poor families, less likely to have sole use of basic amenities, less likely to have had parents who stayed on at school past the minimum leaving age, and more likely to to have a mother who was older than average and worked before they started school. They were also more likely to be female. Some of these aspects of the children's backgrounds are known to affect educational or occupational performance one way or another. So how would the only children fare when we allowed for all these other background factors?

To find out, we used a statistical procedure known as "stepwise regression", which allows us to check whether any of the background factors has an influence on the various outcomes we want to look at and then to see whether having or not having a sibling has a significant effect on these outcomes, allowing for the influence of those other background factors. An effect (or a result) is regarded as "significant" if it is unlikely to have arisen simply through chance. Social scientists usually only rely on results where the likelihood of a spuriously important result having arisen through chance is less than 1 in 20.

The main message of the stepwise regression was that though many of the background factors had a significant effect on the children's performance, "sibling status" (whether or not a child had a sibling) did not, once those other factors were allowed for. The only aspect of performance on which sibling status had any significant effect, allowing for the effect of other background factors, was the reading test at 11. In other words, being the sole child in the family brings only a marginal advantage compared with having one sibling.

These findings from the NCDS are right in line with other recent large-scale studies that have similarly allowed for the effects of background factors. The 1988 review by Polit and Falbo, which we looked at earlier, showed that only children performed similarly to one-sibling children on most measures of ability and achievement, but were significantly ahead of them when it came to verbal ability (which includes reading). In 1983 two Swiss researchers, Ernst and Angst, published an exhaustive review of research on family size, together with a survey of their own. They concluded that once family size and background factors were taken into account, the achievements of only children were comparable to other sibling children, though in their own study male only children were slightly higher achievers.

In a similar study to the NCDS, a US researcher, John Claudy, found that on measures of intellectual ability and educational achievement only children performed better than children from two-child families, but the differences were very slight. Another US study headed by Theodore Groat, this time of adult only children, found that in occupation and income there was little difference compared with sibling children. In 1989 Judith Blake, a leading expert on the effects of family size, drawing on data from no less than six large US surveys dating from the 1950s to the present – a total of 150,000 children, found that only children performed similarly or marginally better than one-sibling children from intact families, once background variables were taken into account. In 1992 a study of Canadian women found that though only children appeared to have higher educational levels than sibling children, this difference virtually disappeared when their parental background was allowed for.

I have taken this rather roundabout way of presenting the results to show how important it is when you are trying to compare only and sibling children to take into account other factors that could also have an effect on the results. If you fail to do that it can look as if differences are caused by lack of siblings, when in fact they are due to other aspects of only children's lives. So as to avoid that, from now on our comparisons will all be between only children and one-sibling children who were with the same two parents throughout their childhood, and for every important result we will also look at whether it is still significant, allowing for other factors.

So at last we come to the answer to the second question: "Does having or not having a sibling make any difference to how a child turns out in terms of ability and achievement?" The answer seems to be "Possibly, but it's very marginal." Whether it should enter into anyone's deliberations as to what size of family they have seems to depend on their own situation. You will remember that families in skilled working-class occupations had a higher proportion of only children, possibly because they wished to give them the entire benefit of what resources were available. When we compared the ability and achievements of only and one-sibling children separately for this group we found that only children were significantly ahead in reading (and hence other language skills) throughout their school-days and were significantly more likely to be in higher status occupations at 23. These findings suggest that in less affluent families where parents themselves have had fewer educational and occupational opportunities, limiting your family to one may give your child a slight boost. It seems the parents who choose to have an only child on those grounds are not making a mistake.

None of this, of course, means that every only child is a marginally higher achiever than every child with one sibling. What we have been looking at are statistical patterns, which talk in terms of trends; the average, the overall pattern. Within those trends there is tremendous variety. Only children and children with one sibling, like all other children, come in all shapes and sizes and in all levels of ability and intelligence. There are plenty of very able and achieving children from large families, just as there are only children with learning difficulties. What the research tells us is not that every only child turns out an achiever, but that not having a sibling does you no harm at all, as far as intelligence and achievement are concerned.

Summing-up

Only children are often said to be above average in intelligence and achievement. Is that true? It depends how you look at it. If you ask how only children compare with the rest of the population, the answer is they do tend to be higher achievers, but that is mainly because children from small families tend to do better than those from large families – you would get a similar result if you compared children from two-child families with the rest of the population. If you ask whether being without siblings makes you a higher achiever, you have to allow for other factors which also have a bearing on the question. Having done that, the answer seems to be that lack of siblings seems to make little difference, if any, to a child's ability and achievement. Whether you have one child or two simply does not matter. What counts is the potential they are born with and the environment in which they grow up.

CHAPTER THREE

Are Only Children
Maladjusted?

"Being an only child is a disease in itself."
(Attributed to G. Stanley Hall)

In the last chapter we saw only children lose the sole advantage they are believed to have. They certainly tend to be achievers, but so do children with one sibling, so it is possible to do well educationally and professionally without forgoing the benefits of sibling company which are considered essential for normal personality development. The case against the one-child family seems closed. But is popular opinion correct in assuming that without siblings children grow up maladjusted?

The Claim

At first glance, there seems to be plenty of evidence to support the belief that only children turn out different from (and in most respects worse than) other children. Judging from books and articles on only children, expert opinion, in the form of paediatricians, psychologists and therapists, seems to be agreed with the popular view that children need siblings in order to develop normally. In 1976 Ronald Illingworth, Professor of Child Care at Sheffield University was quoted as saying "It's not surprising that the average only child, existing as a threesome with the parents, with no one around to compete with for their attention, has an unusual slant on life." While pointing out the advantage only children have in receiving undivided parental love and attention (a loved child usually grows up into a loving adult) he considers that there is a particular disadvantage in that "Only children don't get the early experience of rough and tumble. This is part of life and without it a child is not prepared for school or adulthood." (*Observer,* 5 December 1976)

Child psychiatrist Dr Dora Black is quoted as saying that the presence of a brother or sister creates the first "social laboratory" where children practise sharing, "experiment with relationships and learn to cope with change, envy, competitiveness and rivalry – things that will help them develop social skills," (*She* magazine, May 1992). Diane Jonckheere, a personal development counsellor and an only child herself says only children can be overmature. "As adults, only children either take responsibilities which don't belong to them; or they rebel against taking any responsibility whatsoever ... some of us can take life very seriously. We don't always know how to have fun," (*Independent on Sunday*, 26 January 1992) And counsellors quoted by Pitkeathley and Emerson say that only children are readily identifiable by their need for emotional space, their lack of ability to engage with others or share themselves, and their problems in placing themselves on a "dependency/independency continuum".

Similar expert views have also been found in textbooks on child development, psychology and psychiatry. As long ago as 1922 a psychoanalyst claimed that "The only child is usually spoiled and coddled because the parents gratify all his whims ... This has its evil consequences in adult life, for the slightest deprivation hardly noticeable by the average person, is enough to throw him into a fit of depression and rage lasting for days and even for weeks... It is due to the undivided attention and abnormal love that the only child gets from his parents that he develops into a confirmed egoist ... [he] becomes vain and one-sided and develops an exaggerated opinion of himself. In later life he is extremely conceited, jealous and envious. He begrudges the happiness of friends and acquaintances and is therefore shunned and disliked."

Another authority, Alfred Adler, who is regarded as the founding father of birth order psychology, portrays only children as spoiled by their mothers and competing with their fathers. They want to be the centre of attention and suffer in adult life because they are not. They grew up in an atmosphere of anxiety and are thus predestined to faulty development; inevitably spoilt and incessantly in need of support.

A more recent specialist in birth order psychology, writing in 1969, confirms that the outlook for only children is poor. Male only children are "used to winning acclaim, arousing sympathy, concern, sorrow and the like and getting all possible support on a moment's notice". Hence they tend to feel they should always be the centre of attention both at work and in social relationships. Female only children tend to be capricious, extravagant and selfish, a nuisance at work and a "poor sport" with their colleagues. Both males and females make problematic marriage partners, since they are attention-seeking and unwilling to take responsibility for looking after children. If both partners are only children "They will, with great likelihood, remain childless; the few exceptions tend to prove that they should have."

Contemporary authors also convey a similar theme. An authoritative psychiatric textbook, *Disorders of Personality* published in 1981, comments of only children "Such youngsters often are cherished by their parents as posessions of extraordinary value. Not only are these children fawned over, but they frequently experience few of the restrictions and learn few of the responsibilities of sharing acquired by youngsters with siblings."

With such overall expert agreement it is small wonder that even some books specifically intended to reassure parents of only children can have the opposite effect. *Raising the Only Child* by US paediatrician Dr Murray Kappelman sets out in Chapter 1 to point out that one-child families can have advantages. However, the author is soon bogged down in doom. "The singularity, the onliness of the only child tends to result in certain characteristics that can be found in a high percentage of only children." The only child may exhibit marked independence or dependence, and finds it hard to make and keep friends. He tends to be highly competitive and hence "often finds it extremely difficult to maintain intense and enriching relationships over an extended period of time ... A significant proportion of school phobias, unexplained failures, drop-outs and outstanding students who suddenly cave in emotionally are only children." The one-child family with its "interaction between two dedicated adults and a developing child is obviously fraught with dangers".

Expert opinion seems then to concur with the popular belief that being an only child is bad news; for the child, the child's acquaint-ances, colleagues and partners and for the rest of society. These beliefs can only have been strengthened by recent publicity sur-rounding the effects of China's "One Child" policy. Accounts of a generation of "Little Emperors" struck an obvious chord when they reached Britain. In an article headlined "Fat brats worry the Chinese" the *Guardian* reported:

> China's one-child policy is breeding a generation of overweight and overindulged brats, according to a Chinese newspaper ... One in every 60 children in Peking is obese, which in the view of one expert "makes the children lazy and impedes their mental development". Many of the only children are also characterised as "indulgent, selfish, introverted, unconcerned and unable to care for themselves". (2 April 1986)

A *Times* article agreed. The problems occasioned by the policy, such as enforced sterilisation and female infanticide were minor "compared with the problems that could occur in the future ... The prevalence of only children is already causing problems in schools and special units are being set up to deal with difficult only children. In ten years' time, the majority of China's young people will be only children". (21 October 1985)

A grave prospect indeed, if popular and expert opinion are right. But are they? If so, they should be reflected in research findings. The claim suggests that:

1. Only children are by and large different from people who have siblings.
2. These differences are negative – only children turn out worse than other people.

What does research tell us about these claims?

The Reality

Researchers have been studying only children for at least a century. In the early days, some studies did indeed find that only children were more likely to have problems and this undoubtedly contributed to and confirmed popular and expert opinion. However, these studies have been criticised for not approaching the subject in a properly scientific fashion and hence coming up with questionable results. For example, one of the most famous early studies published in 1898 by a psychologist called Bohannon, found that they were malingerers, did badly at school, had poor relationships with other children and escaped from these difficulties by inventing imaginary companions. In fact Bohannon arrived at these results, not by studying only children directly, but by asking a group of students and teachers to describe an only child they had known. What purports to be an objective study of only children is therefore in reality a study of individuals' memories of only children, which are likely to have been selective. If you already believe only children to have certain qualities and are asked to describe one, you will tend to choose one who fits your beliefs. Bad research often makes good news, though. The study was widely quoted and reported and taken up by US authors as evidence of an "only child syndrome".

In the first half of the 20th century, studies came up with mixed findings on only children, some positive, some negative. Then there was a period of silence. The baby boom was in full swing and only children were thin on the ground. However, in the 1960s and 1970s there was a renewal of interest, especially in psychiatric research. The research takes two forms. First, there are studies of particular groups (schizophrenics, alcoholics, lesbians) comparing only and sibling children within those groups. These studies are usually based on very small samples and hence are not necessarily very reliable. They also only tell us about only children who belong to that group – they do not tell us anything about those who do not.

Second, there are studies that try to establish whether only children are more likely to become members of those groups (more likely to become schizophrenic etc). They often took the form of comparing the proportion of only children among psychiatric patients with the proportion of them in the general population (as judged, for example, by census data). In general they tended to find that more only children than you would have expected were having psychiatric treatment, and they drew the conclusion that only children were more likely than children with siblings to develop alcoholism, neuroses, personality disorders, schizophrenia, drug addictions, psychosomatic illnesses, homosexuality and problem behaviours of various sorts. You name it, only children were more likely to have it.

Ernst and Angst, who have reviewed this research, are highly critical of the methods used in many of these studies. Comparing patient groups with census data is a procedure full of statistical traps into which many of the researchers tumbled. The chief of these was that they failed to allow for the effect of family background, especially of broken homes. Since there is a link between family breakdown and many types of psychiatric disorder, and since only children are more likely to come from broken homes, that could account for the fact that more of them are found among psychiatric patients. Studies where background factors like this were allowed for tended to find that only children were at no greater risk of mental illness or problem behaviour than anyone else.

An alternative way of testing whether only children are more likely to have problems is to take a sample of children and adults from the population as a whole, divide them up into only children and sibling children and then see if there are differences between the two groups. This is the typical form that most recent research has taken and it comes up with a very different picture.

Only children are not different

The first preconception recent research knocks on the head is that only children turn out radically different from other people. In fact, the main finding is that they are strikingly similar to other children, especially those with only one sibling. Ernst and Angst's review of the research up to 1980 concluded that whether or not you have a sibling appears to have little effect on personality or behaviour and another overview of research from the same period by Toni Falbo, came to a similar conclusion.

In the late 1980s Denise Polit and Toni Falbo got together to test these findings out in a more systematic way. They conducted another massive quantitative analysis of over 500 European and North American studies, all of which had compared personality and social behaviour in only and sibling children. The studies varied considerably in quality, which Polit and Falbo allowed for by a formula that gave less weight to poorly-conducted studies based on small samples, and more weight to well-conducted studies based on larger samples and taking account of background factors. They grouped the many personality and social attributes that the studies looked at into 16 categories, based on the kinds of social and personality characteristics that people have supposed to be typical of individuals from different family sizes.

Their most striking finding was that on all but two of the categories, only children scored similarly to children with siblings. That is, they did no better and no worse than sibling children on tests of leadership, citizenship, maturity, generosity/cooperativeness, dogmatism, autonomy, locus of control (feeling you are in control of your life), self-control, anxiety/neuroticism, emotional stability, contentment, extroversion, social participation (in clubs, in dating) and peer popularity. Their finding suggests that only children are much more like sibling children than they are unlike them.

Since then, several other studies have come to the same conclusion. One US researcher, Steven Mellor, decided to test Polit and Falbo's findings for himself. He gave personality questionnaires to a group of children aged 11 to 19 (to approximate the age range of the studies Polit and Falbo had analysed) and found that only children were strikingly similar to other children with one sibling on trust, autonomy, initiative, industry and identity, but that both only and one-sibling children were different from those from larger families. This echoes the earlier study of only and one-sibling children by Claudy, which found few significant personality differences between them. Both these studies made careful allowance for background factors.

Our analysis of information from the National Child Development Study confirms these findings absolutely. There were a number of "ready-made" indicators of personality and behaviour in the study and we looked at them all. They included:

- Ratings of school behaviour and adjustment to school at ages 7, 11 and 16, which teachers completed, and which are designed to pick out children showing signs of psychological disturbance.

- Ratings of home behaviour at ages 7, 11 and 16, which parents completed, and which again are designed to pick out children showing signs of disturbance.

- An "Academic Motivation" scale completed by the young people themselves at age 16, which gave their their ideas and feelings about school and education.

- A " Malaise" questionnaire at age 23, completed by the adults themselves, which picks out individuals at risk of non-clinical depression.

- At every age, information about whether the children/adults had experienced any psychological, psychiatric or emotional problems, and whether they had received treatment for them. This was gathered from medical examinations, from parents, and at 23, from the adults themselves.

Our most striking finding was how little the only children differed from those with siblings.

There was no significant difference between the school behaviour scores of only children and those of one-sibling children at any age, though there were slight differences between those two groups and children from larger families. The home behaviour scores of only children again did not differ from those of one-sibling children. They had similar scores on the test for depression at 23. Stepwise regression showed that, allowing for background factors, sibling status (whether or not a child had a sibling) had no significant effect on any of these items. Only children do not therefore appear overall to be at greater or less risk of psychological disturbance than those with siblings, on the basis of these tests. Nor, with two exceptions, were there any significant differences between only and one-sibling children on whether they had at any stage experienced, or seen a specialist for, psychiatric, emotional or psychological problems.

Although the individual items on the home and school behaviour questionnaires are not designed to be taken on their own, it is worth mentioning that on the majority of them there were no differences between the two groups. Some of the mainstay elements of the only child stereotype were knocked for six. Only children were no more likely to throw tantrums at either parents or teachers. They were no more likely to be worried or anxious or upset by new situations, or withdrawn. According to their parents and teachers they were every bit as sociable and as well liked by other children.

The conclusion from all this has to be that only children turn out very much like others who have siblings – or at least more like them than unlike them. In fact, it appears that whether or not you have a sibling has little or no effect overall on your personality and behaviour.

If you have siblings yourself, or are the parent of more than one child, you may by now be in a state of frank disbelief. When I have told friends and colleagues of the overall findings of recent research on only children they have reacted in the same way. First the gut reaction: "It can't be." Then the search for suggestions as to why the findings may be wrong.

First, they point out that many siblings are widely separated in age. Though two- or three-year gaps are considered "ideal" by many parents, late babies are not uncommon. These "age gap" children would be counted among the siblings in any study, but they would in fact have been the only child in the family for many years. Hence, they might make the sibling group look more like the only children group than it would if it had consisted entirely of closely spaced siblings.

It is a fair point. However, in our analysis it is unlikely to be the whole answer. So as to avoid this complication, we tried to ensure that children whose sibling was very much older or younger than them were excluded from the sample. All the two-child families had to have had two children in the family under 21 at ages 7 to 11 so they cannot have had a sibling more than seven years younger, nor nine years older than them. Given the statistical norm of spacing children closely, the majority probably had a sibling at most four years older or younger. We took similar steps to ensure that children in other family sizes were also closely spaced. So it seems unlikely that wide age gaps could account for the apparent similarity between only and one-sibling children.

The second point people make is that there may be very real differences between only and sibling children which the tests just don't show up. Again, that is a fair point. Personality and behaviour tests are crude devices compared with the complexities of human behaviour.

However, tests do show up differences between other groups – the particular tests used here have shown up very clear differences, for example, between different social classes, between males and females, between small and very large families. It seems likely, therefore, that if having a sibling had a significant effect on a child's personality that would show up as well.

Only children do not turn out worse

The second preconception that research challenges is that lack of a sibling is damaging to a child's personality and behaviour. We have already seen that in most respects only children turn out no different for their lack of brothers and sisters. A more unsettling finding still is that, on the few differences that remain, they are not to the disadvantage of the only children. Polit and Falbo's quantitative study found, for example, that on the two aspects in which only children differed from sibling children – achievement motivation and self-esteem – they actually did *better* than children with siblings. Our NCDS analysis confirms that any differences tend to favour only children. Allowing for background factors, being an only child significantly increased academic motivation at 16. And it significantly *decreased* the likelihood of psychiatric or emotional problems or specialist treatment for them between the ages of 16 and 23. It seems, overall, as if, contrary to popular and expert belief, only children do not have more problems in personal adjustment. If anything, they are marginally *better* adjusted than people with siblings.

Social relationships

However, for many people, all this is beside the point. Only children may turn out to have acceptable personalities according to psychological tests, and it is no surprise they are well-motivated individuals with high self-esteem (aka "pushy and conceited"), but what about their effect on other people? What about their social relationships? How can they possibly make good friends and marriage partners when they have no experience of sharing life and lodgings with brothers and sisters?

The answer is that there is no evidence at all that only children are particularly bad at social relationships. If they were, we would expect to find them shunned by other children and that is not the case. As we have already seen, they have been found to be as generous, cooperative, extroverted, sociable and popular as sibling children are.

Falbo and Polit did find one interesting point in relation to sociability, however. When tests ask only children to rate themselves, they come out as less sociable than sibling children. When tests ask *other people* (such as classmates) to do the rating, only children come out just as well. That suggests that they may see themselves as poorer at relationships than they really are – perhaps not surprising when they are constantly given the message that you need siblings to be a social success. In fact, reviews of the research show that they are every bit as good at making close friendships and just as popular with their peers as children with siblings.

We will come back to the question of sociability in the next chapter, and to marriage in Chapter 6. Meanwhile, it seems clear that, contrary to popular and "expert" opinion, and, indeed, contrary to what many only children themselves believe, growing up with siblings is not an essential prerequisite for getting on with others. Perhaps that is not surprising. The sibling relationship is only one among many that we encounter as we grow up. At the very least only children share a house with one parent, who has his or her own priorities and demands. Away from home they get the same amount of practice at rubbing along with people as anyone else.

Tempting though it is to view siblings as a social gymnasium where you practise your skills before going on to apply them to other people, research suggests it doesn't work that way. Sibling relationships and peer-group relationships are very different kinds of creature, and success in one does not guarantee or even predict success in the other. Perhaps all that getting on with siblings teaches you is how to get on with siblings. You learn to get on with friends, colleagues and marriage partners by making friendships, going to work and being married. And in those enterprises only children have as much experience as anyone else.

The curious case of China

As far as Western children are concerned, we seem to have an open and shut case. Research studies point conclusively in the direction of only children turning out no different (or even in some respects marginally better) in terms of personality and behaviour from those from other small families. You would be hard put to find a well-conducted study that disagreed. But in China, some studies have come out with extremely negative results on the personality and behaviour of Chinese only children. These studies confirmed and strengthened fears about the consequences of a "Society of Little Emperors".

In 1980 shortly after the start of the "One Child" policy, the Shanghai Pre-school Education Study Group compared two groups of four-year-olds – 70 only children and 30 children with siblings. Teachers were asked to rate the children's behaviour. The Study Group found that only children were less cooperative and a higher proportion had bad eating habits, were timid, careless about others' property, hostile to others, unable to care for themselves, disrespectful to their elders and had a "fascination with fancy dress". This study was widely reported both in China and in the West and was influential in forming opinions about Chinese only children.

However, in the same year, two researchers, Dudley Poston, from the Texas Population Center and M. Y. Yu, a family planning doctor, collaborated in research that repeated the Shanghai Study in a different part of China, this time on a much bigger sample of 559 kindergarten children, 196 of whom were only children. The children's behaviour was evaluated by teachers in the same way and the questionnaire followed the same pattern as the Shanghai study. This time the results were very different. On most "undesirable" behaviours, only children were rated no worse than the others, and on some (for example, non-cooperativeness and hostility) they were rated better, although they were still concluded to have poorer eating habits and to be over-concerned with what they wore.

The difference between these two studies is made doubly interesting by the fact that the same thing happened again. In 1986 three researchers from the Child Development Centre of China published a study of only and sibling children in the Beijing area. From a group of 993 children, they matched 180 pairs of only and sibling children on age and background factors. They then asked the children's classmates to pick out those who showed various desirable qualities. They found that sibling children were rated as more cooperative, more competent and more popular than only children. Only children were rated as more egocentric, though also better behaved. The researchers suggested that while only children get all the attention going, sibling children lead communal lives which require cooperation and hence make them more popular and better leaders.

Again, this study received wide publicity, both in China and the West. Such were the concerns in China that Toni Falbo was asked by UNICEF to work with the Child Development Centre to address their concerns and carry out a similar study in Bejing. Falbo says she found it entirely plausible that the outcomes of only children in developing countries would be different from those in the West. To see whether they were, the new study looked at the same range of desirable and undesirable attributes in a sample of 810 7- to 9-year-olds but asked teachers to rate the children instead of classmates. The results were surprising. This time, the only children did as well as the sibling children on most attributes, and better on language achievement and tractability. The results were similar to those of Western studies.

Beijing is a city with a highly educated population, and Falbo considered that the results might not hold true for the rest of China. In addition, the differences between the two studies might be due to pupils and teachers rating children differently. With the help of her University of Texas colleague, Dudley Poston, Falbo carried out a series of surveys in four provinces of China, each with a representative sample of 1000 school children. The surveys included personality ratings by teachers, parents, classmates and the children themselves. Overall, few personality differences were found between the only and sibling children, no matter who rated them, though in one province only boys were rated more highly by their peers.

These results are supported by a slightly earlier Chinese study by William Meredith from the University of Nebraska. This time children themselves were asked to rate their social competence and teachers and classmates to rate their sociability. Importantly, neither teachers nor children knew the purpose of the study until after the ratings were completed. There were no significant differences between only and sibling children, though if anything, only children were rated more positively by their classmates.

So the puzzle is: how can similar research studies come up with such different findings? An interesting fact, which may be completely coincidental, is that the negative findings emerged from Chinese researchers working on their own while the positive findings emerged when they were joined by Western colleagues. Could the Chinese researchers have been influenced by their feelings about the One Child policy, which has been called "The most unpopular and the most widely-resisted policy ever in China" (*Financial Times*, 4 February 1989)? Or could the Western researchers have been influenced by their hopes for the policy in the light of concerns about world overpopulation? Contradictory studies have continued to emerge fom China; some with findings similar to those in the West, others suggesting that Chinese only children have more behaviour problems, according to parents and teachers.

It is puzzling that findings which seem to apply consistently to only children in other countries do not do so in China. One commentator has suggested that Chinese parents who have enthusiatically embraced the One Child policy are different from those who have resisted it by having more than one child; being predominantly young, urban, professional couples with modern ideas. They may produce children whose individuality sets traditionally oriented teachers' teeth on edge. Toni Falbo also points out that Chinese children are taught to introduce themselves in terms of birth order ("second son", "only daughter" and so on), which makes only children highly visible. That could increase the likelihood that teachers' reports would be biased by their own negative feelings towards the One Child policy.

But what is even more interesting than all these speculations is that the negative results from China have been so widely quoted in the British press at the expense of the more numerous positive ones. For example, in 1991 a feature in the *Weekend Telegraph*, which was based largely on an academic article I had published, completely ignored the many positive Western findings on the personality and adjustment of only children, which I had reported and emphasised. Instead it chose to quote much earlier Chinese research findings to make the point that "only children tend to be more egocentric while sibling children are more persistent, more cooperative and more popular among their peers" (17 August 1991).

For the moment, the Chinese puzzle remains. What is important as far as Western parents are concerned is to remember, if you come across them, that the negative Chinese findings have been challenged, and that, in any case, they do not apply to Western children. The evidence that the personality and behaviour of only children in the West are every bit as "normal" and "healthy" as those of sibling children is overwhelming.

Summing-up

It seems clear that as far as personality and behaviour are concerned, there is little to choose between having one child or two. Contrary to popular beliefs and some "expert" opinion, only children are definitely not more prone to maladjustment, mental illness or poor social relationships. In fact they seem to be strikingly like other children from small families. The conclusion has to be that siblings are not essential to the development of a healthy personality and socially acceptable behaviour. How you turn out depends not on your family size but on the genes your parents give you when you are conceived and the environment and upbringing they give you once you are born.

CHAPTER FOUR

Are Only Children Lonely?

*"As we'd roll along, we'd sing three- and four-part harmony, with mother
and dad joining in as soprano and bass ... 'What do only children do
with themselves?' we'd think." (Cheaper by the Dozen)*

The last two chapters have shown that some of the major anxieties
about only children are quite unfounded. Far from being "a race apart"
as many people believe, only children seem to turn out practically
indistinguishable from other children from small families. Far from
making you less well adjusted, there seems if anything, to be the odd
benefit from not growing up with siblings. However, for most of us
that cannot be the end of the story. It is possible that children might
turn out well, but have been thoroughly miserable in the process. An
acute anxiety for some parents and the cause of an occasional twinge of
guilt for most is that their only child may be less happy than sibling
children because they are missing out on the fun and companionship
that brothers and sisters provide. They worry that their child will be a
"lonely only".

The Claim

Looking back, many adult only children seem to agree that loneliness
was a major problem for them. Sally Oppenheimer, a successful
Conservative party politician, told the *Observer* magazine in 1976 that
as a late baby she was much welcomed by her parents. "But as they
were much older and not able to join in with anything, the loneliness
that most only children feel was more intense for me." She was very
bored as a child and hated it, particularly when her parents had friends
round: "I used to have to recite and then sit with them in utter silence
listening to their conversations," (5 December 1976).

In a more recent article, a 26 year old woman explained

> The main problem is you spend loads of time alone. My parents
> were relatively old when they had me and couldn't relate to me at
> all. They never played with me – I think they just didn't know how
> to deal with me ... I was always lonely but I noticed it more as I got

older ... I envy people's families more now than I did when I was younger. Last year I went to my boyfriend's family for Christmas. He has a sister with three kids and it was great – a real family occasion with lots of people around a big table. We used to have a few people for Christmas when I was younger, but it was me, my parents, Aunty Mildred, Aunty Maud, Granny and Grandpa – all of us desperately trying to stay awake for the Queen's speech! ... One sad thing is that now I really dislike being on my own. I feel that after spending so much of my childhood alone, I should be used to it, but I'm not. In that sense being an only child didn't make me self-sufficient. (*Woman,* 24 August 1992)

Christmas is one problem; holidays are another.

We used to spend our holidays in foreign cities. Half the day was spent looking at old churches and museums and the other half was spent doing what I wanted to do. There was a certain rationality to this, but the trouble was I never knew what I wanted to do, so often we would end up spending the whole day looking at museums. If I had brothers and sisters they'd never have got away with this! (*Independent,* 8 February 1993)

Lonely and bored – it's a combination that strikes straight to the heart of Western ideas about childhood. In one study 86 per cent of Australian women considered that "Loneliness affects a child even more than real poverty." While for centuries parents' main concern was that their children should be useful and well behaved, now we believe that they should, above all, be happy. If only children in general are as miserable and frustrated as these extracts suggest, it is a fate that all loving parents would want to avoid.

The Reality

There is no doubt that some only children are bored, lonely and thoroughly miserable and we should not underestimate their distress. But is it true of all or even most only children? In answering this question, we are venturing into relatively uncharted seas. Most of the research on only children centres on how they turn out in terms of intelligence, attainments, personality and behaviour. That area has been well mapped out and we can come to fairly definite conclusions about it. But very little systematic research has been done on how only children feel about their lives and our conclusions therefore have to be a bit more tentative.

A further problem is that "lonely" is itself a complicated idea. The *Oxford English Dictionary* defines "lonely" as "dejected at the consciousness of being alone". That definition neatly emphasises two of the basic elements of loneliness: feeling you are alone and regretting it. For, as most of us know, it is possible to be on your own without feeling lonely, as when you "enjoy your own company" and equally possible to feel "lonely in a crowd". When only children say they had lonely childhoods, they do not mean they were kept in solitary confinement. They seem to be talking about a number of problems.

1. They spent time on their own and did not enjoy it.
2. They spent very little time with other children. This was partly because they had failed to develop the social skills or the confidence to establish friendships with other children – they became shy, awkward and withdrawn. Hence as children, but also as adults, they were also lonely in the sense of socially isolated.
3. They spent much of their time with other adults, notably their parents. This made them feel alone because the company was adult rather than child-oriented; there was no one on their wavelength.
4. These problems resulted in them having less happy lives as children and as adults.

Let us look at each of these points in turn and see whether the research evidence supports them.

Time on your own

Most children from time to time feel fed up and at a loose end and complain they have no one to play with. But is this more of a problem for only children? Common sense would suggest it must be. Sibling children have ready-made companions in the house day in day out. Only children are stuck on their own.

Well, the first thing to say is that only children, like other children, spend a lot of the day outside the house. For the first couple of years, of course, they may well be at home with their parents, but then so will first children, since it is common for couples to wait two or three years before having a second child. Once they are three, most children, only or not, go to a playgroup or nursery school of some sort, where there is no shortage of companions. More parents of only children work before they start school and their children will quite likely be in full-time nurseries or with child-minders, most of whom take more than one child. By the age of five, they are spending half of every week-day at school among teeming hordes of children. Research shows they get on as well with other children as anyone else, so if they are bored at school it is more likely through lack of stimulation than lack of company.

However, it is quite true that children spend more time out of school than in it. What about evenings and weekends? What do only children do with themselves? When the NCDS children were 11 they were asked what activities they did in their spare time and how often they did them. Allowing for background factors, only children spent more time than one-sibling children in "quieter" home-based activities such as reading, drawing, writing stories, painting, stamp collecting and looking after pets. They spent significantly less time on social out-of-home activities such as sports and clubs, though over 40 per cent of all only children took part in some sport on most days and another 40 per cent did so sometimes.

Other studies (for example those by Claudy and Blake) have also found that only children tend to prefer more solitary activities, and that has, of course, led to the suggestion that they are less sociable than sibling children. However, Judith Blake points out that a preference for doing things on your own is a characteristic of children from small families generally, not just only children. Although it is tempting to suppose that only children retreat to solitary pursuits because they do not get on well in groups, the evidence is against that. As we have seen, they get on as well with their peers as children from larger families. The conclusion has to be that it is a matter of preference – many of them just find reading, collecting stamps and looking after pets more interesting than kicking a ball about. They spend time doing things on their own, not because they have no option, but because they want to. So it seems that far from disliking being on their own, many only children, by the age of 11, positively prefer it at least some of the time, as indeed do children with one sibling.

It is, of course, 25 years since the NCDS children were 11 and in the years since then children's lives have changed in many respects. Computer games have probably ousted painting and stamp collecting, and for many children organised clubs and sports have replaced playing in the street. Research into how only children spend their lives today is non-existent. My interviews with only children and their families suggested that their lives are still much the same as those of other small-family children from similar backgrounds. They possibly go to more organised activities (music and dancing lessons, sports, drama and social clubs) either because their parents feel they need the company or because taking them to the activity (and paying for it) is less problematic with one than with two. However, this is simply the impression of the children and their parents; we don't know if it is true.

So the NCDS, like other past studies of how children spend their time, is not necessarily a good guide to what they do now. But what it does let us see is how that generation of only children felt about their lives. And a question to the 11-year-olds about their attitude to their spare time produced one of the great surprises of our analysis. On commonsense assumptions I had confidently anticipated that only children would be more likely to be bored than children with siblings. In fact the reverse is true.

Only children were actually less likely to say that they were sometimes or often bored than children with one sibling, and more likely to say they enjoyed their spare time. A regression confirmed that, even allowing for other factors, being without a sibling made boredom less likely. It is not clear why, but one possibility is that only children, through spending a lot of time alone, get very good at amusing themselves. Children who are used to having a brother or sister around may feel more at a loose end if their sibling is otherwise occupied, leaving them on their own.

Whatever the reasons, research provides no evidence that only children are more likely to be bored or miserable on their own than children with siblings. A small minority may be (4 out of 336 NCDS only children said they were often bored), but the evidence suggests that boredom is not a problem for most only children. Many of the adults we spoke to agreed.

I was good at amusing myself. Either with toys when I was very young or playing in the garden, reading. I had a very strong imagination and so I was able to play by myself. History was quite important to me so I had all sorts of maps and wall charts and things like that. And I had toys like knights in armour, which were metal reproductions. I had a big collection and I played games with them.

[*Did you ever remember feeling lonely or bored, not having another child around?*]
No. I think there were so many things that I was busy with. I can remember saying: "What shall I do?" when I was a bit tired and inspiration failed. That was a slightly trying question to my parents. But it wasn't too often. I was always very interested in drawing and

painting and so that tended to be a sort of focus of my pre-school years, and my father was an artist in his own spare time, and so that seemed a natural thing to do and he encouraged me. My mother, likewise, did because I used to tell her stories about what I was drawing. I can remember standing in the kitchen, painting with my apron on while she peeled the vegetables, telling her about this wonderful world that I was busy painting. I can remember all sorts of activities which I suppose would be just described as play: playing with dolls, making them into families and making them do things and making them go to school and things like that. I think I was fairly happy to amuse myself with these imaginary games. I know I had an imaginary companion. There were also imaginary people who lived in the back bedroom who were supposed to be very wise. I could always ask them about things if in doubt. I think I must have been quite good at amusing myself. I think the fact that I was given ample opportunities: there was no shortage of books and there was always drawing or making. I was also quite keen on things in the garden. I had a little garden patch when I was small and planted cottage mixture. So there were things I could do outside as well as inside.

And this ability to enjoy their own company can persist into adult life:

Looking back on my childhood, I don't have any conscious memories of thinking: Oh I hate this! I never felt that. It actually quite suited, me and even today it suits me to have time on my own when I don't have to conform to other people.

Time with other children

Most only children seem quite happy to spend some time on their own. But few of them want to do so all the time. Like other children, they need friends. We saw in Chapter 3 that only children were no worse at social relationships than anyone else, and our analysis of the NCDS suggests that they spend as much time with friends as other children do. When they were 7, mothers were asked how often their children met friends, other than at school and on the way there and back. When they were 11, the children were asked the same question. The majority of children met with friends most days and only children did so as often as one-sibling children. It is true that slightly more only children said they never met friends out of school at age 11, but this applied to only a tiny minority (5 per cent against 2 per cent for one-sibling children).

Social isolation in childhood does not seem to be a problem then. Nor does it seem to be a major problem later on. At both 16 and 23 there were no significant differences between only and one-sibling children in the frequency with which they went to friends' parties, discos or visited friends and relations, though again there was a tiny minority of only children who never went out.

Overall, this is not a picture of children lacking friends or shunning social contact. Is it in line with other research? Yes and no. Claudy's study which, like ours, compared only and one-sibling children, found that at ages 15–19 fewer only children were dating and that they had a less intense social life. Taking this together with their slightly greater preference for solitary activities, Claudy concludes that only children are less sociable, though he agrees that this does not square with some other research findings. It has to be said that the differences he found between only and sibling children were very marginal and statistically hardly significant. Furthermore, teenage dating is a highly specific kind of social interaction – it might be that adolescent only children are shyer with the opposite sex (though that hasn't been suggested anywhere else) but that doesn't mean they are less sociable in general. And a study by Denise Polit and two of her colleagues of over 500 middle-class married couples with teenage children of their own, which looked at a much wider range of social activities, found adult only children were just as likely as anyone else to engage in sociable leisure pursuits such as voluntary work, helping relatives and visiting friends of the same sex.

It does not seem, then, as if the majority of only children are any more likely to be lonely through lack of friends than others with siblings. Indeed, friendships seem to come as easily to most only children as they do to anyone else, as these accounts show.

> I had friends all the time. I think I was generally liked. I remember at one point through Primary, there were two boys that I generally went around with. Sometimes it would be all three of us together. Sometimes it would be me with one or me with the other but I was always left with at least one of them. I was dead easy to get on with: I generally still am.

> I was absolutely horse-daft from when I was about eight. My cousin had a rather down-market pony trekking establishment, and I spent a lot of time there with friends – weekends, going on holiday, certainly

the school holidays sort of first thing in the morning until about nine o'clock at night – packed lunches and things. There were quite a lot of kids there, some kids I was at school with as well. There were the sort of holiday people that came in, regular people at weekends, but we would do things like catch the horses and tack them and go around on treks and look after little kids and stuff. And we obviously used to go out riding ourselves and take them out to exercise them in between. I don't think, if I would have been asked when I was a child, I wouldn't really have known what people meant in terms of being lonely.

I had luck in having a close friend who I used to play with who was not very far from where we lived. I spent a lot of time playing with him in his garden and we did all the sorts of things that boys do. Games and going out on excursions and being taken to this and that and the theatre and so on and so forth. We went on holiday together. I went several times with him to the Channel Islands for my holidays when I was between say the ages of twelve and fifteen, virtually every summer so that was very enjoyable. That was a close friendship and it still exists.

Time with adults

Only children, like other children, spend some time on their own and some time with friends. Where they differ from sibling children is that they also spend a good deal of time alone with their parents, and, if their parents have anything of a social life, with other adults as well. Whether the family is at home or goes out, sibling children basically have others at hand to relate to on their own level. Only children do not.

That can undoubtedly be a down side of being an only child, as this otherwise very contented 11-year-old points out:

I find when we go out with other adults, because my mum and dad have loads of friends with no children, it can get really boring, because they're chatting, and you're just sitting there.

Though others enjoy it.

I remember I loved being off school. Because it was like my mum and my granny and it was a very female household and friends would come around in an afternoon and they would gossip away. It was very nice because they thought I was terribly well behaved because I would just sit there and read a book, but I was actually listening to everything they were saying.

How lonely is it for only children in adult company? Surprisingly there seems to be no systematic research at all on how only children feel about spending much of their lives with adults, so we do not know how much of a problem it is for them. What I can say, from my own experience and from that of only children I have interviewed, is that it does not have to be a drag.

We tend to think in terms of children enjoying themselves with other children, and assume when only children miss out on this, that they miss out on fun altogether. We somehow discount adults (parents, grandparents, uncles and aunts, friends of the family) as sources of fun for a child. In fact, as most of us have experienced from time to time, adults, if they are so disposed, can make superlative companions and playmates.

First of all, they can share their adult activities with children. Though we tend to compartmentalise children's lives so that they lead separate existences at playgroup, at school, at clubs; even having their own computers and video recorders, this is a very recent phenomenon. In less rarefied societies, children were and still are very much part of the adult world. And until we cordon them off from it, it is a world most children find absolutely fascinating. They *want* to listen in to adult talk, cook the dinner, fix the car. We sometimes find it easier if they don't, but that's our problem. So one way in which children and adults can be on the same wavelength is for the adult to make it easy and interesting for the child to join in.

My father was great with children, he was great fun with me and great fun with other children and so he was terrific company. I used to go sailing with him and I was the crew – I had my own responsibilities on the boat, which he'd taught me to do independently without being told, and I was quite proud of that. And he would talk to me while we were out – he would tell me marvellous stories from history. He had a way somehow of making it all terribly interesting. I don't think I would have preferred being with another child to being with him for that period.

We went out to museums and art galleries a lot. [*Did you enjoy it?*] Yes. It became more and more interesting. But I think they were very sensitive to the fact that I was a child. I can't remember ever being towed around an art gallery in a way that some children are taken around because it was only when I was maybe twelve or thirteen that we began to go around art galleries seriously. It had more been the museum type of thing before then. I think that fitted in very well with my own development so that I wasn't being given something that I wasn't ready for. [*Can you remember how they went about making it interesting?*] We used to talk about what we were looking at, and Daddy could always tell me something about the history, or the story behind it, or explain how something worked, or possibly the artist, how he had got that particular effect or technique or something. But that would be getting on a bit. By the time I was fourteen or fifteen.

It is interesting to compare this quote with the one on page 50. The same adult activity, but a world of difference in how it is presented to the child.

These parents were obviously good at helping their children join an adult world. But, of course, the other way round can be just as satisfactory. When an adult joins in at the child's level, they can both have great fun, as this mother of a four-year-old boy points out:

My dad is his best friend I think. He loves my dad. [*What sort of things does he do with him?*] Just all the wild things. In fact, my friend's wee girl she loves my dad as well. She says: "Where's Grandad? Can I go up to Grandad's?" He's awful good with kids. My boy loves swords and guns and all this dressing up and my dad's just like a wee boy again when he goes up. He's got a lot of time and patience for him. Stupid things – jumping about fighting with swords. He takes them out to the park and up to the wee golf course; takes the football or the plastic golf clubs, tennis racquets or something. Or he goes out on a bike and takes them on his bike. He's very good.

And two adult only children reminisce.

We laughed a lot. My father has a very keen sense of humour and my mother is very ready to join in. I know when I was little there was a lot of playing with Teddy. Teddy would be put on top of a door so that he would fall on top of me when I opened the door and this kind of thing. Just jokes really. Silly things.

My dad had a great imagination. We had all sorts of games we played. My favourite when I was about five or six was that he would pretend to change me into an animal of my choice -- stretching up my neck to be a giraffe, or pulling out my nose to be an elephant. That was the best one, because he'd pretend the nose kept springing back, so he'd end up pulling it across the room and 'nailing' it to the door to keep it in place! Then when I was about ten, we'd make up rhymes to the tunes of popular songs as we went along or silly poems about what we were doing. We always sang together in the car. I remember my childhood as great fun.

Of course, parents of more than one child have fun with them, too. These things are not peculiar to one-child families, though it may be that they tend to develop more readily where children turn to adults for company. We will be looking at parent-child relationships in the next chapter. Meanwhile, all we can say is that only children do not have to feel lonely in adult company. It depends on the company.

Happiness

Despite the fact that, in general, only children seem to enjoy their own company and have enjoyable relationships with their parents and with friends, some researchers have still wondered if, at certain stages in their lives, only children may be overall less happy than children with siblings.

Two researchers from Rotterdam, Ruut Veenhoven and Maykel Verkuyten, surmised that only children might be less happy as teenagers because they were prematurely pressured into adult ways. They collected information from a representative sample of over 2000 13- to 17-year-olds from different parts of the Netherlands, using among other things two different psychological measures of happiness. Allowing for background factors, they found no overall evidence that only children were less happy or less satisfied with life than those with siblings, though teenage daughters of unemployed fathers were an exception to that. On the other hand female only children with working mothers seemed particularly happy and satisfied.

But what about the consequences in later life? Two US studies asked the same question. Denise Polit's study of middle-class couples with teenage children found that the adults who were only children were just as satisfied with life and just as happy as those with siblings. A much bigger and more representative study by two researchers from Texas analysed responses to seven national US surveys, each consisting of about 1500 individuals who, among other things, had been asked how satisfied they were with various aspects of life and overall how happy they were. Allowing for background factors, the results showed that only children were just as happy and satisfied with life as those with siblings and in some respects more so, though none of the differences were substantial.

Our analysis of the NCDS confirms these findings. As we have already seen, at 11 the only children were more likely to say they enjoyed their spare time, and at 16 they seemed more likely to enjoy school. Preliminary information from the latest sweep shows that at 33 they were, on their own assessment, as happy and satisfied with life as those with one sibling. There was no stage or aspect of life in which only children seemed less happy. So the evidence which exists all points in the same direction. Lack of brothers and sisters does not appear to diminish your chances of happiness, either in childhood or as an adult.

It may seem strange that only children's lives appear to be as happy and satisfying as other people's when they are missing out on a human experience which most people would agree can bring great joy. The importance of ties between brothers and sisters is generally accepted, and the sibling relationship has been celebrated by poets and novelists as well as psychologists. How can only children be as happy without it?

There are at least two sides to the answer. First, though we tend to think of the sibling relationship in very positive terms, research over the past two decades has shown that it has its highs and lows. Judy Dunn, one of the founding mothers of sibling research, has shown from her observations of young siblings that while some brothers and sisters are very close to each other and gain a lot from the relationship, others are indifferent or even hostile to each other. Only children miss out on the fun and laughter, but they also miss out on the quarrels and tears. The two possibly balance out.

Second, as Toni Falbo has suggested, there may be aspects of an only child's life which compensate for the lack of a positive sibling relationship. Only children will never experience the love of a brother and sister, but they do have the undivided love and attention of a mother and/or father. Our next chapter moves on to that.

Finally, I must re-emphasise that we have only been talking trends. The research suggests that only children in general are no lonelier and no less happy than other children. That does not mean that there are no only children who are lonely or unhappy. Clearly there are some who are very much so (as, of course, are some children with siblings), though our NCDS analysis suggests that they are a tiny minority. What the research makes clear is that being an only child does not *in itself* lead to loneliness and unhappiness. If only children are lonely and unhappy, withdrawn and isolated, it is not an inevitable facet of their state – it is due to the particular kind of only childhood they have had. Any child is likely to be unhappy if they are ignored, kept from friendships and deprived of the fun of childhood, and only children are no exception. Given good parenting, they are as happy as anyone else. As this father says of his teenage daughter:

> She's very self-reliant when she has to be alone. She reads a lot, she amuses herself a lot, she goes to the cinema or whatever it is. She's perfectly happy alone, but she's also very happy to have friends, so I think both work out. I wouldn't say that one was at the expense of the other, that there is more emphasis on one than the other. She's a very sociable child, that's very obvious. But at the same time, I think when she's alone, she knows what to do. She can amuse herself. She's happy.

Summing-up

One of the strongest beliefs about only children is that they are lonely, socially isolated and unhappy because they lack siblings. Only children themselves often subscribe to this notion and indeed some do seem to be particularly unhappy as children and adults. But there is no evidence that the majority of only children feel any lonelier or less happy than anyone else, nor is it true that they are more likely to be socially isolated. They seem positively to enjoy being on their own some of the time and, surprisingly, are less likely to be bored than other children. They make friends as easily as anyone else and their adult lives appear to be just as sociable. Though some feel a lack of companionship when they are on their own with their parents, others have great fun with them. Finally, there is no evidence that only children are any less happy and satisfied with life either in childhood or as adults.

When only children are lonely and unhappy, it is not because they lack siblings, but because they have lacked good parenting.

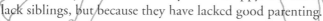

CHAPTER FIVE

Are Only Children Spoiled?

"As a rule, the home treatment has been that of unthinking indulgence."
(E. W. Bohannon)

The Claim

When Michael Ryan ran amok with a machine gun in the suburbs of Hungerford in the summer of 1987, the media were quick to pounce on the fact that he was an only child.

> The brick-built, end of terrace council house in Hungerford, Berkshire, was a permanent backcloth to Michael Ryan's rather dreary life. It was to that building he was brought as the only child of his parents when he was a few days old and it was where he grew up and developed his own fantasy existence ... Michael Ryan received the usual over-attention of a single child, according to neighbours. He spent most of his time with his mother and was jealously guarded by his father ... A family friend described Ryan as a "spoilt little wimp. He used to get everything he wanted from his mother ... he used to beat her up. She paid for his new cars every year". (*The Times,* 21 August 1987)

These reports must have confirmed many people in their belief that only children come to no good. Overprotected, fussed over, pampered, in a word "spoiled"; small wonder they end up "trying to get away with murder".

Are only children in fact spoiled by their parents? "Spoiled" is every bit as complex a concept as "lonely". The *Oxford English Dictionary* reminds us that to "spoil" originally just meant to damage or destroy something to an irretrievable extent. Sometime, in the late 17th century it acquired its other meaning: "To injure in respect of character especially by over-indulgence or undue lenience. Also to treat with excessive consideration or kindness."

This definition seems to fit nicely the various claims that are made when only children are said to be spoiled by their parents.

1. They overindulge them – give them too much.
2. They are overlenient with them – give in to them too much.
3. They are generally too kind to them – smother, protect and fuss too much.
4. By doing all the above they ruin their characters.

How much is "too much"? No one has objectively calculated the optimum level of parental indulgence, leniency and attention. What critics of only children seem to mean is that they are given/let off/ fussed over more than other children are. So let us look at whether there is any evidence that parents of only children treat them differently from parents of sibling children.

The Reality

Indulgence

There are two aspects to this which were well put by one of the couples I interviewed. When I asked them whether they thought they did things differently with their four-year-old because she was their only child, the mother said: "She has a lot more by way of attention. We pamper her." To which the father quickly added "We don't spoil her! We give her love but we don't spoil her with buying nice things."

Realistically, parents of only children do have more to give. They can give their child more material things: clothes, pocket money, sweets and treats, because their income does not have to stretch over several children. They can also give their child more in the way of time and attention, because they do not have several children competing for what is available. So you would expect only children to get more on both counts. Do they?

Money

No one has so far done any research on what the day-to-day life of only children is like, so we know next to nothing about whether or not they get more than children with siblings. However, one of the studies Judith Blake analysed showed that, allowing for family background factors, US sophomores who were only children were more likely than those with one sibling to have had music and dance lessons and to have travelled abroad, though the difference between these two small family sizes was very slight compared with that between small and large family sizes. The finding suggests that both only and one-sibling children get quite a bit more than children in larger families, but that the difference between the two smallest family sizes is not great.

That is confirmed by our analysis of the NCDS. At 16 the young people were asked what their average weekly pocket money was. Compared with all other children, only children got a substantially higher average amount. However, when we compared them with one-sibling children the difference was much less. Only children got an average of £4.88 per week, one-sibling children £4.38, a difference of 50p.

So it seems as if only children may get a bit more than other children from small families, but not as much as you might expect, given that two children double the expense. The reason for this may be that many parents of only children deliberately "ration" their children to keep them in line with their friends, to teach them the value of money and to avoid the dreaded "S word" being applied to their child.

> You wouldn't want to think that she's being spoilt and I'm always conscious of the fact that it could easily be construed that she is spoilt with being an only child. Because of that, you try and go out of your way to make sure that she doesn't really get a lot. She was wanting a bike with the twelve-speed gears and although we could have afforded to get her one, we said "What is the point of you getting one just because other folk have got them? There's no need for it." She's quite happy with the bike she's got, you know? We realise it would have been very easy to just turn round and say she's getting it. Paying for it wouldn't have been a problem, and I feel that, sometimes, she might lose out a wee bit because we're trying not to spoil her.

Time and attention

If parents of only children do not give them that much more than one-sibling children in material terms, they do seem to give them more time and space in their lives. Judith Blake's analysis of the sophomore study showed that only children were read to considerably more often than children with one sibling before they started school, despite the fact that the sibling children could have been read to by an older brother or sister as well as by their parents. Two other US studies found that mothers of only children spent more time each week at home with them and that parents of only children talked with them more at meal times. Our analysis of NCDS data also found that mothers and fathers read to their only children significantly more often at age 7 than parents of two children, and the difference remained significant, even allowing for background factors.

Reading, talking and generally spending time with children is known to further their language skills, and this probably accounts for only children's slight advantages on reading tests. It may also help to explain why, despite lack of siblings to hone their social skills on, they seem to develop personalities that are just as healthy. Parents of only children have more time to discuss the ins and outs of social behaviour and to help their children understand and come to terms with anxieties. One of the mothers I interviewed was surprised at how well her four-year-old had accepted the idea of death.

> I don't know if that's anything to do with being an only child or what. I feel that some of it has to, because if you have lots of children or more than one and you are having to tell them about things it is much more convenient to tell them things that are easier for them to understand at the time. Like Heaven, "Granny goes to Heaven". Whereas I can discuss it with him. We can be rational about it. He can ask me questions if he's disturbed by things. Children need time and space where they can come and ask you questions. That could be easier if you have only one.

Of course, parents of more than one child are also able to talk to them and take time to deal with anxieties. But it may be harder for them to do so, particularly if circumstances are difficult. That could explain why differences in children's language skills show up most clearly in less affluent families.

Leniency

The stereotype of the only child "getting away with murder" seems to fit neatly into theories about discipline and family size. Some sociologists have suggested that larger families are likely to be more authoritarian simply through lack of time – the family becomes "bureaucratised", and parent-child relationships become more impersonal. By the same token, parents in smaller families, especially those with only one child, will be more permissive with them. This is supposed to show up most clearly in adolescence.

In 1981 three US sociologists set out to test this theory. They gave a questionnaire to sociology students, that asked them how much they had been "regulated" by their parents in their last two years of school on a number of issues that could cause conflict between parents and teenagers. On the basis of theory, they expected to find that parents of only children would be rated as less strict. In fact, they found very little difference between the two sets of parents; the only two items on which there was a significant difference was that parents of only children were stricter about their choice of friends and that none of the only children had been physically punished by their parents in the last two years of school. On drinking, smoking, saving and spending, clothes, movies, sports and church attendance, and on pressure to do well at school, there were no significant differences between only and sibling children.

These findings were confirmed in 1989 by a similar exercise with psychology undergraduates, using a different questionnaire, which found that parents of only children were, if anything, less permissive than those with more children. And another US study published in 1990, this time of fourth- to eighth-grade school children, found no significant differences between how only and sibling children saw their parents' enforcement of standards, (for example, knowing what their child was up to and checking if they had done what they were supposed to), or achievement pressure (wanting their child to excel).

Overall, it does not seem as if only children get off with more – in fact, the findings seem to suggest that their parents are as strict with them as any others. This was also what we found in the NCDS. At 11, only children helped about the house as often as one-sibling children. At 16, their parents had similar views about their appearance and were just as likely to ask where they were going in the evening. Parents also appeared no less (and no more) likely to disapprove of their children's friends. In fact, parents in small families seem to treat their children in very much the same way whether they have one or two. There is no evidence at all that, in general, parents of only children are overlenient with them. In fact, a few may do the opposite.

> Certainly my father was terribly concerned I mustn't be spoilt because I think he was even more aware than my mother of the stereotypical ideas of only children, to the extent that if we went out for a walk he would say: "Which way do you want to go?" and I would suggest going one way and he'd say: "No, let's go the other way"!

The fact that two of the studies we have looked at found that parents of only children were no more likely to pressure them to achieve is interesting, because that is an accusation also levelled at parents of only children, not least by their offspring. The "pushy" parent is also part of only child demonology. In fact, the evidence for it is very mixed. True, parents of first children tend to have higher expectations of them when they are young – because they have no previous experience of child rearing, they have rather unrealistic expectations of them and hence are always hustling them along. This possibly has positive effects on the child's intellectual and educational development, but it could be uncomfortable to live with, particularly if they fail to live up to expectations.

> My brother-in-law, my sister's husband, is an only child and I think he led a very lonely life. He doesn't say much but just the occasional things he comes away with. He's quite deep and doesn't show a lot of emotion. But from what I can gather, his father had his life mapped out for him and it hasn't turned out that way. I think he really feels he's been a disappointment. They get on alright but there's that underlying current.

In fact, as we have seen, there is reason to doubt whether most parents do have excessive expectations of their only children later in childhood. The NCDS asked teachers at each stage to comment on parents' interest in their children's education, and their hopes and expectations for them. At 16, they also asked the youngsters themselves how anxious they felt their parents were for them to do well at school. On none of these items were there any significant differences between only and one-sibling children.

That seems strange – you would imagine that having put all their eggs in one basket, parents would be more than normally eager for them to hatch. In practice, it may be that, once again, parents are aware of the dangers and try to guard against them. When I asked one mother whether she had any anxieties about having an only child she said:

> There is this thing – do we tend to put more pressure on him because he is the only one? I hope that's not the case. I know that now he's started secondary education that is the time when it does become an issue. I would like to think that we will let him do what he wants to do but I know that we've got to get the balance between "Come on you've got to do this" and not go the way of "You must do ..." If he's not got the ability, he can't put it there. If he's got something that we know he can do, we can get him to do it. What I feel is that

we want him to do his best but, at the end of it, if he wants to do something else I think you have to say, well, it's his life.

Protection and closeness

On several counts, parents of only children seem more likely to cosset and protect them. An only child is a first child, so parents are inexperienced and worry more.

> Probably just because he is the only one, I worry over the least wee thing. I think probably if you had another one you'd say well, he'd done that, he went through that, but I think when it's your first and your only one you panic more. You're more protective. If he's not well and there's hardly anything wrong with him I'm: "Are you alright?" and I think he knows this now and is getting a bit fly about it.

Because they only have one child to focus on, parents also have time to fuss over them, as this mother of a four-year-old pointed out:

> Because she's the only one, I'll dress her in the morning. If I had another three to get ready she'd be dressing herself. She should be dressing herself ... [*father adds*] She can!

And since only children are also their parents' one bite at the cherry, the anxieties about accidents and bad company that most parents feel can be even more acute.

> I have a paranoia about something happening to him. I have this tremendous fear of road accidents. I don't know what it is within me, but an eleven-year-old, the minute he goes to cross a main road, I'm absolutely ... I don't know if you would have that for every child, but I have this vision ... I know a family friend whose son was killed in a road accident, and I remember ever since then feeling terribly afraid for him. [*Do you let him do it?*] Oh yes. I have to.

That mother handled the situation sensibly despite her fears, but when anxiety gets out of hand it can be very limiting for the child.

> A down-side to being an only child in my case was that my parents were overprotective, which meant that socialising was quite a problem. My father was very selective as to whom I was allowed to

play with. I wasn't allowed to make friends in the street, I wasn't allowed to play on the street. I wasn't even allowed to join the Brownies! So I think I was lonely because of overprotection.

Of course, parents of more than one child also worry and fuss over them as this mother of an only child, who was herself one of three, made clear.

I probably would never let her go anywhere given the chance, but that's just me. My father was the same. We weren't allowed to do anthing in case anything happened to us and that's probably – when we were twelve and thirteen – we were hardly let out the door to cross the road. My mother said he was just so worried something was going to happen.

So do parents of only children in fact cosset and protect them more? There is very little evidence either way, because there are no studies of day-to-day parenting in one-child families. The only research that I have found which refers to overprotection is a Canadian study of the records of children attending a psychiatric clinic for 5- to 12 year-olds. The records showed that in most respects only children were no different from sibling children at the clinic, but their parents were more likely to be rated by staff as overprotective, in contrast with sibling children whose mothers were more likely to be rated as rejecting. However, the researchers point out that at best these findings only apply to children attending psychiatric clinics, not to only children in general.

The NCDS doesn't offer any direct evidence either, but one finding might suggest that overprotection of only children is more likely. At age 7, teachers were asked whether the children were overdependent on their mothers. Although only about a quarter of children were considered over-dependent, the proportion was higher for only than for one-sibling children. Even when we allowed for other factors which might have made dependency more likely, such as mother's age, parents' educational level and social class and the child's gender, being an only child still increased the chance of overdependency as rated by teachers. So it does indeed look as if some only children are more likely to be overdependent on their mothers to a greater or lesser extent at age 7, though the majority are definitely not.

Unfortunately, we do not know in what way the children were overdependent – presumably it could range from children needing their mothers to tie shoelaces, to refusing to be parted from them at the school gates. But it does tie in with the idea that only children are overprotected by their parents and consequently slow to learn independence. It also fits the common belief that only children form abnormally close relationships with their parents, from which they have great difficulty in extricating themselves later on. Is there any truth in that one?

Most studies suggest that "overclose" relationships with their parents are not a problem for the majority of only children. There is some evidence that children in small families have slightly closer relationships with their parents than children in large families. But another quantitative review by Toni Falbo and Denise Polit (this time of 19 studies on parent-child relationships) found that there was no significant difference in closeness between only and one-sibling children.

That conclusion is partly supported by our NCDS analysis. The 16-year-olds were asked how well they felt they got on with their mothers and fathers. Although only children seemed to feel marginally more positive than sibling children, the difference was not significant. However, when they were asked more specifically about potential causes of disagreement with their parents, a significant gap did emerge. On most of the areas mentioned: arguments about friends, clothes, late nights, going places, homework, smoking and drinking, only children felt they had fewer disagreements with their parents, and when we totted them up to give an overall "parent–child agreement" score, we found that only children felt they had considerably fewer arguments, not only than all the other sibling children, but also than children with only one sibling. Even allowing for other factors which had a bearing on these parent–child disagreements (girls had fewer arguments than boys, middle-class children than working-class children), being an only child made disagreement with parents less likely.

That result could be taken two ways. It could be argued that only children have warmer, more egalitarian and rational relationships with their parents, which avoid potential flash points. Or equally, that they identify with their parents to such a degree that challenging them is not a possibility. The Canadian study we looked at earlier on suggested that for children attending psychiatric clinics, the latter explanation may be true. Though the only children did not differ much from sibling children, they were more submissive, and the authors link that to overprotective parenting. They point out that findings that apply to children in psychiatric care do not necessarily hold true for only children in the general population. However, they query whether submissiveness is in fact bad for children, pointing out that it may have contributed to the only children's low delinquency rates.

It is a good point. On the whole, close and harmonious parent–child relationships are considered good for children, and how "overclose" is defined depends on the culture you live in. A relationship regarded as suspiciously smothering in Britain might be considered normal in southern Italy and obligatory in parts of China. It is a curious reflection on our society that close involvement with the two people who brought you into the world is considered a problem. However, there is no evidence that the majority of only children are overprotected, even by UK standards, despite the fact that their parents may be under more temptation to protect and cosset them. Again, that may be partly because parents are aware of some of the dangers and try to hold back, or even deliberately to foster independence in their children.

Is "spoiling" bad for children?

It seems that some aspects of popular beliefs may be true. Although parents of only children do not seem to be any more permissive with them than one-sibling children, nor indeed significantly closer to them, they do spend slightly more money on them, give them more time and attention and possibly also have less acrimonious relationships with them. A few parents may also overprotect their children, though there is no evidence that there is a problem for the majority.

The stereotype assumes that all this is bad for children. Having money spent on them will make them demanding and selfish, having so much time spent on them will make them attention-seeking, and overprotection and overcloseness will make it hard for them to establish independence. Is that true?

Well, it clearly does not have a detrimental effect on their personalities; we have already seen that only children turn out more or less the same as children with one sibling. Nor does it seem to affect their ability to relate to other people – we have also seen that only children are as good at that as anyone else. But do they find it harder to break away from parental protection? Are they more dependent on their parents in adult life?

The evidence seems against it. Our NCDS analysis suggests that by early adulthood they were as independent as anyone else. If only children were more dependent on their parents, you would expect them to stay on at home longer than other young adults. That was not the case. Allowing for background factors, the only children were no more likely than one-sibling children to be still living with their parents at 23. That does not give a picture of only children still tied to the apron strings.

There is, however, one way in which "spoiling" may affect only children – ruining not their characters, but their waistlines. For the "fat brat" part of the stereotype does seem to have some research foundation (though, according to Toni Falbo, it does not apply to only children in the USA). In Europe several studies have found that only children are more likely to be overweight than those with siblings, and Ernst and Angst, who are not given to uncritical acceptance of research findings on only children, concede that this one seems to have some validity. Only children are also taller and start menstruating earlier, both of which are linked to higher levels of nutrition.

Our NCDS analysis confirms that only children are more likely to be overweight. Using a measure of "relative weight", which calculates the percentage by which an individual is over or under their ideal body weight for their height, and allowing for the effect of background factors, we found that sibling status had a significant effect on the likelihood of obesity. Although at most only about 1 in 5 only children was overweight, the percentage who were was higher than that for one-sibling children at both 11 and 16, though it was particularly noticeable at the earlier age. By 23, however, there was no difference between the only children and the others.

It is not entirely clear why only children have this tendency to put on weight. The most obvious explanation is that they get and eat too much fattening food, including sweets. This gets indirect support from a small US study of 5- to 11-year-olds, which found (to the authors' surprise) that only children had more decayed, missing and filled teeth than those with siblings. However, one British study found that although only children were more likely to be obese and ate more of most foods, they had lower intakes of carbohydrates and sugar than children with siblings. (The authors suggest they may have been on diets.)

Another study of childhood obesity by two researchers from Switzerland and Sweden suggested the situation is more complex than that. For girls, heredity and lack of exercise seemed to be the main causes of being overweight. For boys it was overeating and environmental conditions. "Markedly inactive" only children from lower-class families were particularly likely to be overweight in early childhood – they failed to lose their pre-school plumpness as other children did.

That last conclusion is interesting because it is in line with our findings from the NCDS. Although only children in general were more likely to be overweight, when we looked at the social class groups separately, we found clear differences between them. In the middle-class and unskilled groups, only children were no more likely than one-sibling children to be overweight at any age, and they played sports as often. However, in the "skilled working-class" group, only children were significantly more at risk of obesity, particularly in the case of boys, and both boys and girls played sports less often. That tends to support the idea that lack of exercise could also be a key factor in only children's tendency to be overweight.

Obesity in childhood and adolescence is a concern because it can predispose you to health problems in later life. One study has found that adult only children are more at risk of hypertension (high blood pressure), and though there could be a number of reasons for that, too many goodies and too little exercise leading to too many inches round the waist may be among them.

Summing-up

Are only children spoiled by their parents? It depends what you mean by "spoiled". Their parents are certainly not more permissive with them, nor on the other hand do they expect more of them than parents in other small families. Children in small families generally tend to have close relationships with their parents, but only children seem no closer to them than those with one sibling, though they may have fewer disagreements with them. Only children do have more money spent on them, though not as much as might be expected, and they do get more of their parents' time and attention. However, that does not seem to have an adverse effect on their personal and social development. Although a few parents tend to overprotect their only children, this is not a problem for the majority and only children appear just as independent in early adulthood as other children from small families. It seems that most parents resist the temptation to "spoil" their only children, partly because they are very aware that that is precisely what other people expect them to do.

It does seem that only children are more at risk of being overweight in childhood. The reasons are not entirely clear, but it may well be due to them getting more fattening food and less physical exercise. However, this seems to be a problem only in certain families, as the majority of only children are not overweight. Sensible parents do not "spoil" their children in any sense of the word, whatever number they have.

CHAPTER SIX

Is it Harder for Only Children to Cope with Life?

"I enjoyed my childhood but I think there were periods when I would have welcomed brothers and sisters. As I grew older, because my parents were from abroad, I felt that it would have been nice to have some extra moral support in the difficult periods ... to have had a brother or sister to share feelings, and what was going on really."

So far, the evidence has been kind to only children. There seem to be no major disadvantages to being an only child, though there are a few minor pros and cons. However, while the overall trend suggests only children are well off by any standards, people have argued that there may still be certain situations (such as adoption or lone-parent families) in which being an only child is a less happy experience. Only children are also believed to face particular difficulties in relation to certain aspects of life such as marriage and parenting. Furthermore, many only children themselves feel that at particular points in their lives they would have welcomed brothers and sisters. In times of stress or crisis, that is when the value of a close, supportive relationship really becomes apparent.

So is there any evidence that absence of siblings makes it harder to cope with life? There is a problem. If in some previous chapters we were in relatively uncharted seas, here we are in mid ocean "with only a star to guide us by". There is not much research evidence on any of the questions we want to ask, and on some there is none at all. We therefore have to be very tentative in any answers we give, and much of this chapter is speculation.

Marriage

Adults who have brothers or sisters sometimes find it hard to understand how only children can adjust to marriage; and if they are married to one, they may believe that this is a major cause of their difficulties.

> They're ghastly to live with: it's because they've never been teased. They've never had to share the attention; never had the rough and tumble; never been told to pipe down and give someone else a chance. They go through life thinking the big parcel under the Christmas tree must be for them. (*Independent on Sunday,* 26 January 1992)

Only children may be equally critical of themselves as marriage partners. Two US academics, Sharryl Hawke and David Knox, who are both one-child parents, asked about 50 married only children whether not having siblings had an effect on their marital relationship. The majority said no, but just over a third said they had problems in compromising, expected too much attention, or were torn between parents and spouse. Unfortunately, since the researchers did not interview a similar group of married adults with siblings, we do not know whether these problems are peculiar to only children, or whether they are just part of the "rough and tumble" of marriage.

If only children have particular difficulties in partnerships you would expect them to be slower to marry and more likely to get divorced. Is that the case? The research evidence on only children and marriage is very mixed. In the 1950s and 1960s, psychologists who were interested in the effects of birth order claimed that success in marriage depended on it duplicating previous power relationships between siblings. Marriages were more likely to be successful if the birth orders of the partners complemented each other. Hence, for maximum chance of success, an older sister of a younger brother ought to marry a younger brother of an older sister, and so on. On this basis only children would make poor adult partners, since they cannot be complementary to anyone. Birth order theorists tested this idea and found, among other things, that only children had higher divorce rates. However, as Ernst and Angst point out, their studies were often based on very small or biased samples, for example asking groups of adults in therapy to comment on their parents' marriages. Furthermore, they did not allow for the fact that only children are more likely to come from broken homes. Since there is some evidence that being the child of a broken home makes it more likely you will get divorced yourself, that could account for the only children's higher divorce rate.

And in fact three other larger, more recent and more representative studies suggest that only children have no particular difficulties in relation to marriage. Ellen Gee's research, based on a representative sample of over 1200 Canadian women, showed that though only children tended to marry later than sibling children, this difference disappeared once their parents' educational and social backgrounds had been taken into account. And Theodore Groat's analysis of a large-scale representative study of over 7500 married women found that the only children were no more likely to have had a previous marriage. John Claudy's research, which was also based on a large and representative sample of over 3200 young adults of both sexes, and which excluded children from broken homes, showed that the only children were just as likely to be married by the age of 29 as one-sibling children, and, if anything, slightly less likely to be divorced.

All in all, the balance of evidence does not suggest that marriage is any more difficult for only children than for anyone else.

Bringing up Children

It has been suggested that growing up without other children in the house is a poor preparation for having them yourself. You have no first-hand experience of babies.

> Prior to having Martin I had absolutely no idea what having a child would be like. I had never been near a baby before. I had never done any babysitting. I didn't know what to expect and I was quite shocked when I realised the amount of hard work.

Nor do you have any experience of managing more than one child.

> Also, however loving they may be as mothers, only girl children have another hurdle to clear. If they have more than one child, they will find as I have done with my two small boys, that they have no direct experience in handling sibling rivalry and squabbling. (*Observer*, 5 December 1976)

Hawke and Knox asked their adult only children whether being an only child had an effect on their relationship with their own children. This time, two-thirds said it had. Irritation at the children's bickering or at having them around all the time were two problems mentioned, but other parents felt there had been positive effects – allowing their children more independence, enjoying the relationship and valuing their children more. Again, since Hawke and Knox did not interview a comparable group of adults with siblings, we do not know whether the problems mentioned are specific to only children, or just those any parents face.

There is little or no evidence either way. The only research I have found that touches on the subject is Denise Polit's study of married couples and their teenage children, which we looked at in Chapter 4. The researchers asked the teenagers to answer questions about their mothers' and fathers' relationships with them and their behaviour as parents. This included items such as inconsistent discipline, permissiveness, possessiveness, control through guilt and "instilling persistent anxiety", acceptance and positive involvement with the child. According to their teenage children, there were no differences between the parents who had siblings and those who did not.

That does not suggest that lack of experience of young children in the family while you are growing up makes it harder for you to be a parent yourself. In some cases it may do, but there is no evidence of a general problem. Adults who have siblings also find the first baby a shock to the system, and are driven up the wall by constant quarrelling. We should remember that many sibling children have little experience with babies if, for example, they are the youngest in the family, and that only children can learn about babies and about parenting more than one child from their involvement with other families. Almost a half of all NCDS 16-year-old only children had engaged in activites with young children – babysitting, helping with children at school or in a playgroup or in other families.

We do know that only children tend to want smaller families and that they are slightly more likely to want an only child themselves. That may denote a preference for a "quieter life" and less tolerance of the noise and bickering of several children. It may equally be because they enjoyed being an only child and want to do the same again. Unless their partner wants a larger family and neither of them is able to compromise, it is hard to see preferring to have only one child as a major life problem.

Looking after Elderly Parents

Now we come to the real crunch. Almost every adult only child I interviewed mentioned having to care for elderly parents single-handed as a significant disadvantage of being an only child.

After my father died, my mother turned to me for a lot of moral support. Being rather a solitary person of course she had no one to turn to. So there was the sense that she was very dependent on me. So for nineteen years it meant going down south in the holidays and seeing her. And I think then I would have liked brothers and sisters to share the burden of looking after her and doing things.

When my father was ill some years back, I did feel very much how vulnerable you were in a way. You felt there was a sort of responsibility that had suddenly come on yourself. I think that there is that feeling that there is more responsibility on you than there would have been if you had a brother or sister to share with.

My mum has rheumatoid arthritis and she doesn't keep that well, so I tend to help her, which I don't mind at all – but you tend to think if you had brothers or sisters it would help. Somebody helping her as well as me.

The fact that it is harder coping with a dependent elderly parent if you are the only one seemed to me so obvious that it hardly needed saying, let alone researching. However, old habits die hard and I thought it worth seeing whether there were any studies of carers of elderly relatives which documented the additional stress that only children face. In a search of recent British research I found three studies that referred either to the problems of only children or to the role of siblings in providing mutual support. The results astonished me. They were put most clearly in the very first piece of research I looked at – a study of 41 daughters in their fifties and sixties who had been caring for their mothers at home:

Siblings are often regarded in the abstract as additional pools of caring support. However, our data provided considerable evidence of fierce sibling rivalry and bitterness. In contrast, only one respondent expressed bitterness at being an only child. Three of the 20 only daughters expressed the unsolicited view that while they had initially wished they had someone else with whom to share the burden of caring, they now felt the arguments over who was to do what could have been too great.

A larger study of 306 elderly people and their carers selected randomly from six GP practices in Sheffield did not refer directly to only children but noted many examples of carers' resentments at siblings not helping; few instances of siblings being helpful. And a study of 137 supporters of confused elderly people living at home commented that only children felt they had little choice and so just got on with it. In contrast: "However willing, daughters and sons who were not only children typically felt resentful towards their sisters and brothers." In effect, it seemed that one sibling was usually left with responsibility for their parent, the others didn't do much to help (sometimes not even visiting or enquiring about them), and this just added resentment to the burden the supporters already carried.

It seems that the idea of brothers and sisters all mucking in to share the care of their elderly parents is something of a myth. In which case, only children may be no worse off than anyone else, except of course that siblings have a one in two (or two in three, or three in four) chance that they will not be the one who does the caring. And only children certainly escape the practical and emotional complications, as a few of the adults I spoke to recognised.

My mum was ill at the beginning of July. She had to go into hospital for an operation and this time I really felt a heavy load because of Tim. Trying to fit in two visiting hours a day when you have a just under two-year-old was hard work. I kept thinking, if only I could phone a brother and say: "Will you go tonight? Would you go this afternoon?" And even when she was out of hospital: "Would you go and get some messages," and I thought: This is the challenge of being an only child. That you don't have anybody else to do that. Having said that, my husband is one of three: one girl and two boys. At the moment, his maiden aunt is not well and his sister has been complaining that the two boys never do a thing. In actual fact, I do more as a 'niece-in-law', if you can call it that, than either of the two boys do, so I suppose I could have had two brothers and be saying: "The two of you never go near mum!" So, I don't suppose it's really got a lot to do with being an only child. That is a stress thing then because not only do you think, "I have to do this", but, "Why are they not?" Whereas I do not have anybody to resent. It's a case of either I do it or it doesn't get done. End of story. To me that's a fairly simple thing to cope with.

I think there are advantages even in terms of parents getting elderly: like my mum has just put her name down for sheltered housing. I think it was a lot easier because I just said to her "Make an appointment with the solicitor, I'll come", and we got things sorted out. Whereas I think if I had brothers and sisters they might not have the same perspective as me and they might be saying "Oh I don't think you should be encouraging her to do that," So in some ways it's easier because there is just me.

So is caring for elderly parents really no more stressful for only children? The only study to answer this question directly comes, as most only-child research does, from the USA. Two researchers used data from a large scale survey to look at carers of 683 elderly parents in frail health who needed help with at least one aspect of daily life. They looked both at the amount of time carers spent in looking after their parents and at how stressful it was for them. They found that the bulk of parent care tended to fall to one child, and, not surprisingly, that daughters did more than sons. Comparing only children with sibling children, only sons spent more time than sons with siblings in caring for their parents and also experienced the most stress. In contrast, only daughters, though they spent even more hours in caring than only sons, felt under less stress than daughters with siblings.

The researchers are unable to say why this should be, but one plausible explanation is that, in our society, men are typically not expected to care for elderly relatives; that is "women's work". So only sons, who have no option, resent it, thus feeling more stress. The women who are currently caring for elderly relatives belong to a generation who expected to take on that role; they therefore feel less resentful about it. In addition, the close relationships that many only children have with their parents may help them to feel positively about caring for them later in life. As one adult only daughter said to me: "I would be only too glad if I could somehow help, because they've helped me so much."

It seems then that for women of the current generation of carers, being an only child is not in practice a disadvantage when it comes to caring for elderly relatives (though it may be seen as such by some). It does seem to be more of a disadvantage for men, possibly because they are obliged to take on a role which they are not comfortable with. Young women of the late 20th century, who have grown up expecting equal rights to a full career, may feel similarly at a disadvantage when it comes to their turn. That said, much must depend on the relationship between parent and child.

On your own in Later Life

Many people believe that for only children, the worst part will be towards the end of life.

> One feels a need for that missing link ... There is no one of the same generation with whom to talk over childhood days, no one to say "Do you remember when ..." and there is no brother or sister to give any support or advice in times of crises. (*The Times*, 24 June 1987)

Is it really worse in later life without brothers and sisters? We simply do not know. There has been no research on elderly only children, and we can only pick up clues from other research on ageing. On the one hand, there is evidence that people grow closer to their siblings as they get older, which suggests only children lose out. On the other hand, there is evidence that they also grow closer to other relatives such as cousins, and to friends and even neighbours, renewing old friendships and making new ones. Only children have as much chance of that as anyone else.

The main importance of brothers and sisters in old age seems to be in the shared memories they carry for each other. They seem to be less important as a source of practical help or emotional support – most elderly people turn to their partners or children or to friends for that. So, the answer probably depends on what your situation is. If you are unmarried or married with no children and you have few friends, then siblings may make a crucial difference to your sense of well-being in later life. If you have a spouse, children and childhood friends with whom you can share reminiscences, and new friends with whom you can share your life, then brothers and sisters would probably play a secondary role anyway, and whether you have them or not may make much less difference. As at all stages of life, the sibling relationship, important though it can be to those who have it, is only one of many. There is no evidence that without it only children are bereft.

Lone-parent Families

As we have already seen, many only children grow up with only one parent. If, in the popular view, being an only child is bad, being the only child of a lone parent is even worse; possessive mother and overprotected child cut off from the rest of society. Even some researchers who are convinced that only children in general come to no harm consider that they may still be at risk in a one-parent family, with the combined dangers of overinvolvement, isolation and confusion over gender roles. If that is true, there are an awful lot of very vulnerable children about – the number of only children who will spend some part of their childhood in a one-parent family is increasing throughout the Western world.

If you are a child in a lone-parent family, is it in fact a disadvantage to have "no forest of siblings into which [you] can run and hide", as Dr Murray Kappelman suggests? Do only children suffer more in these circumstances than children with siblings? The evidence is mixed, to say the least.

Hawke and Knox's study of parents of only children included about 30 who were lone parents. They appeared to have a range of views on their situation, some finding it particularly difficult, others not. But because Hawke and Knox did not interview a similar group of lone parents of more than one child, we cannot tell if these views are peculiar to the one-parent/one-child situation or just those of any lone parent.

A US study by Weiss, which included interviews with both groups, did suggest that life in a lone-parent family is worse for only children. A lone parent focuses more on one child, which can have a negative effect: the child receives all the resentment going as well as all the concern. The child can become oversensitive and overinvolved with the parent's anxieties. And the fact that parent and child depend on each other can make it hard for the parent to be in control when this is appropriate. Mothers may begin to regard their only sons as more of a marriage partner than a child, leading to sexual overtones and ambivalence. Mothers of only daughters can feel themselves in competition with them and jealous of their social success. Overall, Weiss's message is that this is a less healthy situation than if there were more children around.

However, as Weiss himself says, his book is based not on systematic research but impressions from a number of studies each of which was non-representative of single parents as a whole, and he states "It would be unjustifiable to suppose that our materials provide a base for statistical generalisation." They are useful for understanding some of the situations that can arise in one-parent/one-child families, but not for deciding whether those situations are typical of all such families and whether they differ from those in one-parent families with more children.

That is a point also made in another more recent small study of 24 families whose teenagers were in-patients at an adolescent psychiatric unit. The researchers found that the 12 one-parent/only-child families were more disturbed than the other 12 families who were either lone parents with more than one child or couples with one child. However, they point out that we cannot assume that these findings are true for all one-parent/only-child families.

For that we need a different sort of study – one that is based on a representative group of lone-parent families and compares the situation of only children with that of sibling children in a systematic way. The only study to meet those criteria was carried out by Denise Polit. She compared 47 one-parent/one-child families with 43 one-parent/two- and three-child families, as well as with a smaller group of 20 two-parent/one-child families. All the lone parents had recently been divorced. She used both checklists and in-depth interviewing techniques to gather information on a variety of topics. She found that the one-parent/one-child families had fewer financial problems and functioned more smoothly – partly because childcare was easier and the mothers were therefore able to find work more quickly. The only children appeared to have adapted to the divorce as easily as children with siblings and had no more emotional or behavioural problems. Although it is assumed that siblings will support each other after their parents divorce, Polit found that was rare – in the two-child families particularly, children tended instead to vie for their mother's attention. The only-child mothers tended to be positive and optimistic in outlook and to feel more in control of their lives and Polit suggests that these qualities may have been passed on to their children.

Denise Polit's findings were mirrored in some research I carried out in 1989, analysing information from a large representative study of Scottish youngsters who were in their last compulsory year of school in 1985–6. Lone mothers with only children were more likely to be in full-time, better paid work. Possibly as a result, their children were slightly less likely to have truanted, more likely to be finding life very worthwhile and more likely to have stayed on in full-time education than those with even one sibling.

Clearly, the evidence on one-parent/one-child families is mixed. However, it seems to point away from the assumption that only children are especially at risk in lone-parent families. As Denise Polit says, "Although the findings are tentative ... the burden of proof regarding the extreme 'vulnerability' of only children in single-parent families lies with those who have made the claim."

Adoption

As we saw earlier, being adopted is one reason why a child may end up as the only one. In the past, it seems to have been relatively common for couples to adopt or foster one child, but times and opinions changed, and by the 1950s they were being warned against it. Cutts and Moseley, who in 1954 published the first book on only children, are, on the whole, reassuring to natural parents who have one child. However, they do not recommend that couples adopt only one – parents are naturally anxious about adopted children, they say, and their anxiety is multiplied by that over having an only child. Result: overprotection. For many years, on reasoning such as this, adoption agencies deliberately tried to place at least two children with every adoptive couple. Now that there is an acute shortage of babies free for adoption, couples often have to settle for one. Is that indeed harmful to the child?

Yes, according to Stephanie Siegel, author of a recent US book on adoption, based on her experiences as an adoptive mother of three and as a counsellor for adoptive families with problems. At the end of a long chapter of advice on how to help adoptive siblings get on well together, there are two pages on "The Only Child". They tell parents who have chosen to adopt one child of the "unique needs of the family with the only child". Such parents have a more limited perspective, and hence "expectations may be based on unrealistic ideas". Focusing on one child may place a greater burden on them: "What starts out as involvement and caring often ends up as overindulgence and smothering. An adopted child who is an only child has more problems to solve when he is showered with affection and rewards." Over-idealising adopted children creates conflicting feelings in them that can spill into other relationships, and "Only children are more prone to these inner tensions." Children like this tend "to have poor peer relationships, feeling alone and never fitting in" and turning instead to their parents for friendships. This prevents parents fulfilling their authority role in the family and their "son or daughter will become confused and insecure and more perplexed about his or her self worth and identity".

Doubtless Dr Siegel has encountered one-child families like this in her counselling practice. But the overall effect of these pages is to imply that they are typical of adopted only children and that adoption is more problematic for only children. Is that so?

Not according to a study of British adoptees by Lois Raynor published in 1980, which selected a representative group of 160 adopted children and traced them when they were young adults. One third were only children, one third were the eldest, and one third were at least the second child in the family. One of the aspects Lois Raynor looked at was whether a child's position in the family affected how the adoption had turned out in terms of the satisfaction of both adopters and adoptees.

> A question which often exercises adoption committees is a child's place in the family. Should all adopters be encouraged to take two children? ... Overall [family place] had not been an important factor in the group under study. Although several adoptees had longed for

brothers and sisters, in fact the proportion of "only" children who were satisfied was the same as for those with siblings.

She found that the adopted only children seemed as well adjusted as those with siblings and that their parents were just as satisfied with how the adoption had turned out. She concludes that overall the presence or absence of siblings bore no relation to how the adoption turned out. Much more important were factors such as parents accepting the child as fully their own and striking a good balance between attention and independence.

This is only one study, but it suggests that although some adopted only children have problems (as of course do some adopted siblings), they are no more likely to do so than anyone else. There seems to be no evidence that the adopted only child is more at risk. Success or failure of adoptive placements does not depend on the number of children in the family, but on the way parents handle the situation.

Disturbed Families

We saw in Chapter 5 that only children tend to have good relationships with their parents and that this could account for the fact that they tend to do well despite lacking brothers and sisters. But as one study points out:

> Obviously, not all parents love, accept and interact well with their children. However, it is the only child who is most vulnerable and susceptible to the family environment, good or bad. Siblings can act as a buffer and may accept a person when the parents do not. If the only child's parents are warm and accepting – fine; but what if they are cold, aloof and insensitive?

The idea that children with brothers and sisters are better able to cope with parental abuse (in its widest sense) is a common one. The above quotation was prompted by the finding that lesbians who were only children were more likely to have been sexually abused, rejected and isolated in childhood than lesbians with siblings (though they appear to have been as well adjusted in adulthood). The researchers draw the conclusion that only children in general may be more vulnerable to disturbed parenting.

Some experts agree. A clinical psychologist quoted in the *Guardian* (28 February 1994) says: "It's damaging to be the butt of a disturbed parent if you have no ally." And a psychiatrist quoted in the *Weekend Telegraph* (17 August 1991) says he has "often come across cases of abused children whose brothers and sisters have been a lifeline". At an intuitive level that does make sense – it must be worse to be the only focus of abuse, with no siblings to protect or comfort you. But we should be wary of assuming that this is the case. We know that in cases of child abuse other children are not always helpful – they may condone the abuse of their sibling, exacerbate it by scapegoating and bullying them, or even abuse the child themselves. The above study does suggest that for a particular group, an abused childhood was worse without brothers and sisters. But there appear to have been no studies that compare the experiences of a wider group of only and sibling children in disturbed families, and we therefore simply do not know whether in general they are worse places for only children than for anyone else.

Siblings and Support

It may seem extraordinary that only children in practice face no more difficulties in coping with life, when many of them feel siblings would have been such a help. One reason may be that children who do not have them have an idealised view of the part siblings play in life. When things are not going well, it is tempting to suppose they would have been radically different "if only ..."

In fact, preliminary analysis of the latest sweep of the NCDS casts an interesting light on the role of siblings as sources of emotional and personal support. The 33-year-olds were asked who they would turn to for help in a range of problem situations. In the three situations where emotional, as opposed to practical, help was needed, only a small minority of one-sibling children said they would turn first to a relative, (which will have included brothers and sisters). It seems that siblings are not usually the preferred port of call in a crisis, even for those who have them. Most of the sibling children said they would turn first to their partners, or where the difficulty was with that relationship, to their parents or friends, as of course did the only children. If that is the case, only children are in fact as well endowed with sources of support as anyone else.

Summing-up

We have looked at a number of life events which are popularly supposed to be harder for only children to cope with. The evidence is very limited and in some cases non-existent. Overall, it does not seem as if lack of siblings makes much difference. On present evidence, only children seem to be no worse at marriage or parenting than anyone else. Although caring for elderly relatives is regarded as a particular problem for adult only children, this seems true only for men; paradoxically, female carers who are only children may actually be under less stress than those who have siblings. There is no evidence as to whether being an only child makes it harder to cope with ageing.

Nor does it seem that being an only child makes you more vulnerable in special family circumstances. Only children in one-parent families appear as happy and well adjusted as those with siblings, and so do only children who are adopted. Although it has been suggested that only children are more vulnerable in other unhappy family situations, there is no evidence of this.

Whether or not you have brothers and sisters does not seem to matter very much when it comes to coping with life. Siblings may be a support in difficult circumstances, but there are many other more important factors which help people to cope, such as their own personal resilience and the quality of their relationships with parents, partners, children and friends. Only children are just as likely to have those as anyone else.

CHAPTER SEVEN

Looking back with no Regrets

In the last six chapters we have examined the claims that are made about only children, and shown that most of them are unfounded. Only children in general not only seem to be as well adjusted as those with brothers and sisters; they are, by their own accounts, every bit as happy and satisfied with life. Yet there is no doubt that some adult only children who appear to have turned out fine still regret their lack of siblings.

That is not, perhaps, surprising. If you live in a society where nearly everyone else has something you do not, you are likely to feel you have missed out; and even more likely to do so if society keeps telling you that the thing you lack is an essential part of life. But there must be more to it than that. While some people do regret being an only child, others do not. Though there is no research evidence as to what the difference might be, my encounters with only children over the years suggest to me that the two groups may in fact have had very different types of childhood.

We have looked in previous chapters at some of the things that go to make an only childhood a good experience. To sum up and illustrate the point, this chapter presents the lives of three of the only children I interviewed who said they had no major regrets. It is worth noting that I had no trouble finding them. In fact I have chosen these three simply because they happen to be the oldest people I talked to, and they therefore have the longest span to look back on. There were others who had equally positive things to say. I suspect that there are more unregretful only children around than we think, but that we just don't hear from them.

The accounts they give have been shortened from much longer interviews, but I have kept to their own words and to the spirit of the interview. In particular, I have been scrupulous about including every negative comment they made about being an only child.

Margaret

Margaret is a widow in her early seventies. She was brought up in a small town on the outskirts of a major city. Her father was a cinema manager and her mother had been a tailoress before she gave up work to get married. Both parents came from big families who lived locally, so Margaret had lots of cousins nearby, and spent a good deal of time with them.

My mother, perhaps because she had an only child, was the one that did all the visiting around the family. The rest of them had too many to bring with them. She would suddenly say, "I think we'll go and visit Aunt Jean tonight", so we'd just get ready and go. I had plenty of folk to play with when the grown-ups wanted to sit and blether, so that was quite good. I particularly remember times with one set of cousins – there were nine of them! We used to go on picnics and a great thing to do was to go to the park on a Sunday because nobody had Sunday work in those days. We used to go there for family picnics and play at French cricket and that sort of thing. We used to get the tram through to the park. They were great fun.

I also did lots of things on my own obviously because we weren't out visiting cousins every day of the week. I loved reading. I read a lot. I would get into all sorts of positions to read, perhaps lying on the couch and then all of a sudden I'd think to myself, "I'm not comfy", and before I knew where I was, I had my elbows on the ground and my book or paper on the floor and the rest of my body up on the couch! Maybe the brain worked better in that position! At one time I had piano lessons and tap dancing lessons – that sort of thing. But I was very self-sufficient in that way; it didn't worry me that there was nobody around to play with. On the other hand if somebody came to door I would chuck the book and go. Playing round about the area, roller skates and what not. I had groups of friends round about. In those days there weren't all that many cars, therefore people weren't nipping into cars and away. There was always somebody playing about.

Also I did a lot of things with my mother during the school holidays. We went to museums and parks and always went to the zoo at least once during the summer holidays. I did that with my children as well. I used to love taking them to the museums, things like that.

I was lucky perhaps with the fact that my father had a decent job. On the other hand, I didn't see him all that much during the day, but before I went to school I used to be put to bed in the afternoon so that my father could see me when he got home at night. I always had a wee sleep in the afternoon so that I wouldn't be all sleepy and girny when he came home at about half-past eleven at night. I saw him then. Just for fifteen minutes or so, but he always liked to see me when he came home.

I got on with my parents very well. I don't remember having rows or anything, my memories are all good. I don't have anything that I can say I was annoyed at my mother for doing, or my father or whatever. So we must just have had the odd tiff and that was forgotten about – nobody kept things up.

[What did you do when you were all together?] We played games like cards, like snap. And then of course in those days of no television, we listened to the radio, played gramophone records and then every now and again, we'd have family get togethers and end up with about 20 people in the house! All telling stories about what they used to do, and do you remember this and do you remember that. I used to love it, because I was very often the only youngster there. That never occurred to me before now, but I can remember sitting listening to all the stories about what so and so did and what they got up to themselves and that sort of thing.

There were also quite a lot of good singers in the family and the family gatherings we used to have were great. They were all fairly musical, whether they could sing or whether they played. I had an uncle who was absolutely marvellous. He could play anything, whatever you put down in front of him. Or if you hummed over a thing to him that he'd never heard before, he could accompany you and pick up the key. He was like Les Dawson, he could play all off key! It was so funny! Marvellous! We'd sing around the piano.

And we'd play at things like cards in the hat. It was a bowler hat and you had a paper about the size of what the *Express* used to be, quite a big paper, and the hat in the middle of this, and you had twelve cards and you had two teams of four. You started off, say you were standing here and the hat would be over there and you'd throw one card at a time and in the hat was three points, on the brim two, on the paper one. So you threw your twelve cards and everybody did the same and everybody got points and the next round was two cards at a time and the next round was four at a time. My father was great at that, he what he called "labbed them in". One, two, four, eight and twelve and it was great if you got all twelve in at the one time and you'd get extra points for that. Then all the points were totalled up and which ever team won got a prize. There's many a laugh we've had at that.

[Did being an only child make any difference to your life?] The only thing I would say on looking back is that I was very lucky to be able to go on holidays with my mother and father where a lot of people couldn't go because their families were bigger and they couldn't afford it. We went to places like Scarborough and Bournemouth and Llandudno. In those days, before the war, that was a distance to go. Whereas lots of folk were just going to Rothesay. It was just me and my mother and father, but that was fine because you usually met people in the hotel and you chatted to them and there were youngsters there and you'd play out or play table tennis and what not in the hotel. I really thoroughly enjoyed that and I didn't think there was anything strange about going just the three of us . That was just the way it happened. [Did you make friends easily?] I can remember being very shy to begin with, but once I got going, we bletheied and played away fine, no problems.

I really had a good childhood. I enjoyed it I must say. I can't look back on anything on my youth that I was really hurt about. All I do know is that I didn't get everything that's piled on the children nowadays. I suppose if my parents thought a thing was good for me to have they would see if they could possibly get it at some time or another, but if you really wanted anything bad enough you would save for it. I've always taught my two the same.

[*Were you quite close to your mother?*] Yes. I never thought anything about it, but it must have been an automatic thing. We were there together and we went out together. She must have felt a bit of a draught when I started going out with girlfriends, but she never passed any comment on it. The girl I was going out with or the boyfriend were always invited for their tea and then we'd go away to the pictures and she would sit and listen to the radio. Mind you, I knew that if I was going to be late I had to phone home to say where I was and why I was going to be late, that kind of thing. My mother was always very protective. She never went to bed before I came home. I was a bit like that with my own two.

Apart from two short spells away, Margaret stayed at home working in the school meals service, partly to be with her mother.

She had diabetes actually and she was alright for quite a while and then she would sort of go down again. I think it was because I was away; really and truly I do. Although I was home every weekend she didn't like the idea of me being away. So I came back into the school meals service here and I stayed at home till I was married.

Three years later Anne was born and then a year and a half later, Ian. So that just fitted in nicely. [Did you ever think of having just one?] No. Never planned anything. I'm a great believer in just take what comes! It saves a lot of arguments. If somebody says "I think we should go somewhere", I don't immediately say "No, I don't think we should go there, let's go somewhere else!" I just say "That's fine". That's me.

My mother was dead before I married. I stayed on with my father and then when we got married we all lived together till he died. My father got on great with the children – they loved him. He was a great help to me with them. He was able to look after himself to the end. It was just a very sudden heart attack that took him. I missed him terribly. [Do you think that was worse because you were the only one in the family?] Well, by that time I had my own husband and the two children, so that everything went very peacefully really. I missed him very much certainly, and so did the wee ones because they were so fond of "Papa", but even now, I think of things that he did and have a wee smile to myself. He had a good sense of humour. So did my mother, a great sense of humour.

Looking at it now, I think I would have been quite happy to have had a brother or sister at my age, because you don't have many people of your own age group to talk to. This cousin of mine is the only one I could possibly confide in if I wanted to relieve my mind of anything; now my husband's dead. My friends tend to be telephone acquaintances now – they've all got their own families to think about and they move away and so on and so forth. I still keep in contact with them by phone and Christmas cards etc. My cousin's the only one. But then I was quite happy earlier on because I had the two children myself, and enjoyed every minute of their growing up, I must say. I miss them now that they're away. But my daughter's not far. She pops down a couple of times a week and my son's in the United States; he phones about twice a week. They're very good.

My cousin and I got together again a couple of years ago. She's on her own now, too. We have great fun. We just sort of took up. It would be round about the time of her daughter getting married, invitations going out to the various folk, and you tend to keep things up after that. We did; we kept up very well. It's great now, when I'm on my own again and she's on her own, too. You can just go to the phone and say "Would you like to go somewhere?" and we just go! We just took up conversations as if we'd met the day before – we just seem to think more or less in the same way.

I couldn't say there was anything wrong with being an only child. I would imagine it would depend very much on the parents, if they've got time for their child. Maybe now with both of them working a lot of them don't. But I had a very nice childhood. I don't ever remember having any terrific arguments with anybody. [You're an easy-going sort of person?] Yes. And my parents were the same of course. They must have had their arguments when I wasn't within hearing, because everybody has, but I was never aware of anything. They were great.

John

John is a professional man in his early fifties. He is married with two children – he would have been content with one, but his wife was keen to have more. He grew up in a rural community where his father owned a small farm. His mother developed heart problems, and so his father left farming when John was nine, and went to work on the railways. Both of John's parents came from large families themselves.

My mother was late-ish in life having me. I think that having to work hard on the farm, she'd lost a number of babies, she'd had miscarriages, so that was one reason why she was a bit late in life having me. And then at the age of thirty five she started with angina so she was advised not to have any more children, which she didn't mind because she found it quite a problem having a child in her thirties anyway!

The interesting thing about that was that it was war time and we had evacuees that came to stay with us, and the woman of that family kept the house going, relieving my mother of pressure. The youngest of their sons was about fourteen years older than me. The house was full of people, I suppose the circumstances of the day. So I was as much amongst them as with my parents.

By the age of nine, that had all come to an end because those evacuees had moved off, so then it became quite a quiet life. But I think after that I always had a lot of friends. I didn't feel I had to go out and cultivate them, they were just there in the village community. I can well remember there were one or two who were quite close friends but there were always others and there was always something going on. So I never really felt alone at all. I suppose I was always a bit of an organiser. There were always boys in – making things. [What sort of things?] Anything. We'd make anything! From electrical experiments to the usual wooden buggies and what not. There was a boy at the village mill who was a bit like an only child because his two older sisters had left home, and he and I really played a lot together. The old village mill was an excellent place and we had a workshop there. We had a lot of space to do things, and I think that was primarily because it was a village background. In a sense I was the reader. I was the guy who went off to read the books to find out how to do things and then all this other lot joined in!

We all seemed to be occupied most of the time. I suppose, in a rural community in those days, there was a certain amount of time taken in the summer in hay-making, with the kids helping the adults in one way or another.

There again, I was involved with the air cadets quite a lot when I was older, which was another important thing. It did get us out of the country scene and we went off to some RAF place, and there was flying and shooting and all sorts of, for boys, fairly interesting things. That was another good influence. So that when I came to leave home to go to university, I had been away quite a lot and worked out how to survive amongst contempories.

I didn't do very many things with my parents because being older they didn't perhaps identify with the younger age group so much. My father wasn't very good practically, so he couldn't make things, and I think I discovered as a child I needn't go to him to repair anything – I had to do it myself. There were one or two occasions when my father played cricket with us. It was a disaster! But most farmers are like that. He was an archetypal farmer of the day. Most farmers, and I think still today, don't play with their children much.

My mother was the one with a lot of initiative. I didn't notice it at the time, but when I think back and see how she tried to relate to me when I was quite a young child, it was almost mature in many ways. I can re-member going to things like the pictures with my mother and we would go and see quite mature things that she wanted to see. I used to sit fascinated. I think it would be rather unusual for a mother to take a child like that then. In the country anyway. But you see although that is more or less entertainment, in my mother's mind, part of it was educational.

In some ways I was always conscious of my mother being harder on me than other parents with more children in the family. I think she was determined that I wasn't going to be spoiled in any way, and certainly some of my cousins were much more spoiled than I ever was. They always had more toys than I had. I think that was part of her determination that I was one only child that definitely wasn't going to be spoiled. I'm sure it was a conscious thought process of my mother's. Similarly, from a very early age I was brought up to be cautious about money and handle it well. There again, it always seemed to be that there was a deal involved. If I wanted a bicycle, I had to raise so much first. That was once I got beyond a certain age. That was part of encouraging responsibility. I still retain that.

I think what galled my mother in my early teens was that I wouldn't work at school. She had this vision (she'd never had any higher education) her son was going to have everything she could possibly arrange, and she'd go out of her way, including pursuing me with a sweeping broom, to make me do homework. The broom would connect on occasions! We had some stormy times. But I think once I got to university and established that I was serious, we got on extremely well. [Was that her expectation of you that you would do that or was she just hoping?] She was just hoping. I don't think she had any defined plans of what it would result in, and I think I probably exceeded all those in due course, but she was always a good encourager. The only knowledge she had was what she read and native intelligence. It was really the understanding of an intelligent country woman – if she didn't know it she'd go and read about it, and in a way she didn't fit too well into some of the village communities because others suspected her of knowing too much, or whatever. She was a bit outspoken as well, of course.

She was always reading. Anything. There were always books around the house. She was a lay preacher as well you see, so she was always studying. I remember her working on sermons and things and reading for that. I think in some ways what I achieved was a projection of what my mother wanted to achieve but was never able to do. In that all that her father could think about was work. All the family had to work rather than go into further education, no matter whether they were quite intelligent or not. In the modern scene, there's no doubt that she would have been a person of authority, perhaps in a university. She'd always wanted to be a librarian.

[*Did you feel under pressure because of that?*] To some extent, but no I shouldn't say that. I was under pressure when I was at school, and rightly so. She discerned that as the normal, quite regular teenage male I would do anything but take study seriously. Certainly from my twenties onwards I related very well to my mother. We had a very similar temperament and I think we got on very well. It got to being a very honest relationship really.

John did get to university and started work in a town some distance from his parents. They died when he was in his late thirties and still unmarried.

My father died first. He was a bit older. That was the only difficult time, the six months when he was bedridden after a stroke. My mother was looking after him during the week but I was going there for weekends and looking after him over the weekend and then going back to work. It was pretty hard going. [*Do you think that would have been easier if you'd had brothers and sisters?*] I don't know, because again, the village community helped out. The incredible thing is, there were some farmers who were doing their own farming work during the day, and then coming and staying the night with him to help out so my mother would get relief. Tremendous.

My mother died two years after him. Fortunately I was there. She had a heart attack and died fairly quickly. That was quite hard. One of my old friends in the church, a person I respected very much, he said something which was quite poignant but I would take it from him. He said: "Look, you're an orphan now." And it's true. I was and the sort of tussles I was having were that. I didn't feel deflated by the comment. I thought, well that's a correct summary.

So, again I suppose, a number of aspects came in there. With having connections still with the rural community, because I inherited these farms, I had to keep on relating to them and that was in a sense one anchor stone. The other was some cousins and so forth. And neighbours, the people in the farm next door, who, after my mother's death, whenever I was up there, they would have me in for breakfast. It was quite difficult to break this in due course. That became part of it – I was just taken on board. A man in his thirties. I've had some good friends over the years. Both male and female. I think I've been very fortunate with that.

[*Have there been any times when you've wished you had brothers and sisters?*] No. Never. I've never thought about that, no. But I've been trying to trace back in my mind to some incidents which might be significant, which may indicate it. This family that we had as evacuees – obviously in early years they had quite a big influence, at least the mother whom I call "Auntie". When they left our farm they went into the local town first of all before they moved back to the north-east of England. She was always very kind, and in some ways I benefited from some aspects of her. But the reason I was trying to recall this to mind was that when I was nine or ten I had been staying for a few days' holiday with her and with her youngest – in some ways I think I had in my mind that he was my older brother. So I'd gone home and said "I'm going to take all my savings out and go and live with Auntie." I remember my mother sitting down and explaining "You belong to us. You're our child and you've got to live with us." So the thought had run through my mind that there was more going on in somebody else's family.

[*Has being an only child made any difference to the way you are?*] Yes, I think it probably will have. Although in early childhood the house would be full of people, I very much got used since about the age of nine to having a quiet house. I find that quite difficult now, having a young family. I can't get anywhere where there's silence if I want to do any reading or any work in the evening. There's always this going on around, which I don't take very easily to. So yes. I think again when it came to undergraduate work and having to study hard and swot for exams, this ability of being able to just sit in a room on my own for hours and hours and hours became quite a key thing.

I think that in some ways I was very privileged to be an only child. Having said that, there might be one thing, if you could call it a disadvantage, but it may not have come from being an only child but from somewhere else – the country background or maybe my parents, perhaps my mother. It is that I have always been very wary of people. Maybe I was taught to be wary of people until you knew them better. I think maybe that affected my relationship with women, for example, in that I was always very careful not to get too involved for a long, long time. Maybe that's why I stayed a bachelor for so long. I think if I'm honest, that came from something back there. And this thing of not revealing too much about yourself. In other words, you don't commit yourself in any personal thing. I think that may have its origin somewhere either in being an only child or in coming from a farming community.

But I suppose I have benefited in many ways from being an only child. This boy I played with from the village mill, his mother, although she was a widower, for the eleven-plus, got him some private coaching from some guy who'd been director of education and had to retire early. So, a little later on, my mother decided it wasn't going too well, I was enjoying wasting my time, and of course, O levels were coming up and I was nowhere near getting through them. So she had written to this guy and asked him to help to coach me for O level you see, Maths and English. I don't know if I responded very well, but we did stay friends across many years as a family. The interesting thing is – and this is perhaps what I link on the only child thing – much later, one of my colleagues who'd been an only child had had the same guy to help him through entrance exams to a Catholic school. I would think the same thought process had gone on there in all three families – the widow, my parents, and the family of this other boy. All folks without any real understanding of the methods of education, just some desire to make it happen for their child.

Jean

Jean is in her late sixties, a retired education officer. She grew up in a small mining village in central Scotland. Her father was an engineer in the local colliery; her mother had been a cook before she married. Both parents came from small families; in fact Jean's mother had been orphaned and brought up by her grandmother as the only child in the house. Jean lived next door to another family with three girls slightly younger than her, and the four girls virtually grew up together. Many of the extended family also lived in the village.

[*Do you know why you were the only one?*] No. I've thought a lot about it and I just wondered if perhaps, you see I had no children, and never did anything not to have children, so my mother may have been a bit subfertile too.

I don't think it would have made any difference how many children my parents had – you see, they were people who gathered children to them. I had a cousin, Helen, and she and I were always awfully close. She spent as much time in my house as she did in her own. The three Blackstock girls next door, as toddlers, would arrive round with pyjamas tucked under their clothes and say "Mummy Armstrong, I've come to stay." I think my mum was a kind of incipient kindergarten teacher.

One thing that has always impressed me, and looking back I'm even more impressed, who taught them to bring up children? I don't think they set out in a planned programme to say "This is how we're going to bring up our daughter." I think it was like Topsy; it just grew. It was something that was natural to them. Because the other thing I can remember clearly was that our garden was always full of children. My mother would call and say: "OK kids, the surprise today is ..." and we would try to guess, but what she was doing was she had gone and made up a mixture for pancakes and we all queued up and ate the pancakes as they came off the girdle. My father painted part of the kitchen wall a dark, dark, green so that it could be a blackboard. From when I was about three or something I remember chalking on this part of the wall and playing schools and things with other children. He drew peever [hopscotch] beds for us on the kitchen floor with chalk when it was wet, and all my friends would come in and we'd all be playing in the kitchen.

The house was an absolute centre for everybody. Mother would say to Dad: "We haven't seen the so-and-sos for a while. Let's have a kipper party! Let's have someone different in the house." Everybody got soldiers of toast and kippers – she did that kind of thing. So our home was very much a social centre.

So we were a family that opened up. We went to town, we went to the theatre, we went every year to the pantomime. They were both very literate, both loved the theatre. My father was very knowledgeable about the countryside and walked with me and the Blackstock girls every day. We learned about the birds in the trees and the wild flowers. There were always reference books in the house, always encyclopedias, but no money.

I think they were quite indulgent with me. Not with money, because we were quite poor, but indulgent because we had a lot of laughs. They were indulgent with my stupid daft turns that I used to do at night times. I'd pull my pyjama trousers up and put on my father's tile hat, and then there would be all this laughter. So that was indulgence in a way. It was fun.

On the other side of the coin, it was a very happy relationship, but I know they were critical of me. It must have been hell for them when I was going through the ordinary stages of the teenage years – the black and white and no grey. I can remember my father saying, "Supposing I have to crawl on my hands and knees up and down the River Almond", which was just at the bottom of our garden (he made a garden gate and we could walk it), "I'll never go on holiday with you again!" I've never forgotten it! I must have been about fifteen or sixteen and going through the awkward stage. They maybe wanted to go putting and I didn't want to go putting, so I was being difficult. So there was criticism. It was no one hundred per cent indulgent-only-child-thing. There was criticism. And I did the naughty things like lying and smoking brown paper up the chimney. It was a very normal childhood.

And I was a normal teenager. I remember I desperately wanted this curly white lamb coat, and I said to my mother, "I just love this coat", – I can remember as clearly as anything I said "It's the one thing in life I would like, Mother." They were always absolutely honest and she said "We can't afford it. It would be lovely for you to have it, but we can't afford it." And there was a girl at school who was also an only child. Her people had a pub, a lot of money and there was a great deal of material indulgences, and I used to envy her because she could get things, and I learned very quickly not to say what I wanted to have because she immediately got them. She got the white coat and I remember crying, and my mother said to me "Well, I explained to you that we couldn't afford to buy it for you" and, I think this is sweet of her too, she was obviously trying to help me over my traumas, she said to me "And anyway, Molly Perrie's coat was bought with whisky and beer money. Many of these men go in and spend their money in the pub and there will be nothing left to feed the children on when they get home." So that was her kind of help over the stile of disappointment, wasn't it? To say, this is the moral issue. Yours is the envious issue but here's the moral issue, this may help you to get over it. Neither of them would ever identify their actions or their philosophy in any professional way. It was obviously a natural talent that they had.

I had always wanted to be a school teacher, but when I was sixteen I decided I wanted to be a hairdresser, and my mother said, well that was perfectly all right, but what had happened to all the years of playing schools, had I changed my mind? And I said "Well, I just love to do hair." I think she was terrified I was going to be a hairdresser when she must have known that I was going to be all right as a teacher and that I would probably be a bit bored after a time with hairdressing. But she was wise enough not to push too much. She just said "Do your extra year at school and see how you feel." Our English teacher was qualified to take us for the first year of teacher training and we were farmed out to all the village schools round about – very good preparation! And of course once I was there, it was marvellous. I didn't change my mind in any way after that.

Then, when I was seventeen, and it was the long holiday before I was to go to college, my mother said "Have you thought that you might like to get some experience of life out and about – a holiday job to get some experience of how other people live?" It hadn't occurred to me, that was early days for people taking holiday jobs. So she said "I'll tell you what we'll do. We'll look at the *Scotsman.*" And there was a job advertised. I had a holiday post for 13 weeks. I was paid one guinea each week to look after six boarding school boys. This Mrs Finlay had given hospitality to five boys who, for some reason or another couldn't be with their parents during the summer – perhaps abroad or family problems or what not. So I was paid a guinea a week and she'd made one of the big bedrooms into a dormitory for six beds, and we went fishing and played cricket and I patched their trousers. It was a wonderful summer! Now that was my mother's suggestion.

Jean completed her training and started teaching, but she stayed at home because she enjoyed it.

I never thought of getting a flat of my own, it never occurred to me. [*You were happy at home?*] Absolutely! I was having a great time – dancing, entering jitterbug contests (I was quite popular as a partner). My mother said once "There's not another man coming into this house that I'm going to feed, unless it's the man you're going to marry! I'm fed up entertaining!" Because I didn't marry, you see, until I was twenty eight or twenty nine.

Joe was a widower whose wife had died five years previously of cancer. I met him through mutual friends. We were both on the same wavelength and we liked the same kind of things and I met him in the December and we were married the following June. And my parents and Joe were an absolutely astounding and closed-shop trio. Absolutely, and my parents would come to stay and Joe would say: "Oh, don't bother going home this weekend, just wait until next weekend" and so they really got on terribly well. Before I met him, my parents didn't say anything, but God help them, I could have made some terrible disasters with some of the men in my life.

Jean was happily married for thirteen years. Then her husband and her parents became ill and all died within a few years of each other.

Mum and Dad were both ill and Joe was ill and that was a bad four years. It was Joe first, then my father, and then my mother. That was the whole family. But I coped and I think that I maybe coped because – I don't know, maybe it was pre-training. I had been well experienced in disappointments – I didn't get my white coat! I suppose there were other things that they would just say quietly to me "We'd love you to have that darling, but we can't afford to buy it."

I'll tell you one thing about an only child: when push comes to shove, you've got full responsibility. There's no help. I'm not saying that's a disadvantage, but the only child should get more kudos instead of being thought of as the spoiled one. They should get more kudos for how they cope in stressful situations because there is no brother nor sister to share the responsibility in relation to parents. It never occurred to me at the time, but I'm just thinking about it now. I may have felt it easier if I'd had brothers or sisters who would have shared the support of my parents (because I had to support them financially too, the rates and taxes and things like that). An only child has to do that because there's no other person alongside. But I didn't mind it. I didn't mind it at all.

Eventually mother went, of her own choice, into a nursing home. That upset me. She had made the decision. She didn't want to burden me, I think that was it. She knew I had to work because of course I had no pension, and she and our local doctor decided together that they would get everything sorted out and then they would tell me. So she decided to go into the nursing home, and I was terribly distressed about that because I felt that I was letting her down and what would people think? That I wasn't going to look after her. However, she [had] decided. Then I went through every weekend to see her. I stayed with my friend Isobel and her husband; they were marvellous. I went to see mother on a Friday evening and we spent the evening together: we maybe played cards. Saturday morning, after breakfast, I went and collected her and we spent the whole day together and then I would go back to Isobel's house after tea. I would see her on Sunday and then come home and I did that for all the time she was in the nursing home.

I remember saying to Isobel, when mother died, "I think perhaps I've been helped in each of the three occasions I've lost someone, because I haven't been left with a guilty conscience." That's nothing to do with only children, I suppose. Except, an only child could be made to feel very guilty. My parents never did anything to make me feel guilty. They always were appreciative when I did go and see them. [*It sounds as if, in a way, they were encouraging you to be independent, rather than being over-protective and possessive?*] I think you put your finger on it. I hadn't really crystallised in my mind that all of the time, although we were very close, they were saying "Get out and get on with it". That was it.

I think my whole life has been conditioned by the fact that I knew my parents liked me. Even in the midst of rows and everything else. I wouldn't change it. I don't think, looking back, I don't think I would want brothers and sisters the second time around. I would choose again to be an only child with lots of experience as I had of playing with children who were living in the village and meeting their parents and getting all their experiences and eating soup in their house and having them eat soup in my house. [*Do you not feel some regrets now that you're older?*] No. Although it would have been nice, I think, to have somebody to have shared the support of Mum and Dad, I did it and there was no problem, and maybe I was just tired the times I was saying it. But I don't know whether that's because I have such good friends. I now see no need for sisters because my cousin in America, she and I have always been close, we were very close as youngsters, sister-like rather than cousin-like. I have a very nice close and very loving family relationship with another friend in Dunbar. And the three Blackstock girls, who have been such a big part of my life from their birth, are really almost surrogate family because they look on me as their older sister. So whether it's surrogate or not it doesn't matter, if the feeling is right it doesn't matter. I have no regrets. No regrets whatever.

CHAPTER EIGHT

So, Why the Myths?

Only children present a paradox. Popular opinion sees them as lonely, maladjusted and spoiled; research evidence shows them to be as sociable, well adjusted and well brought up as other children from small families. So how did this gap between myth and reality come about? How has a group of people who seem to do well by any standards acquired such an unsavoury reputation?

Like other types of prejudice and misconception, the origins of the only child myth and the reasons for its remarkable staying power are hard to pin down. Researchers have put forward a number of possible explanations, all of which are pure speculation. It seems unlikely that any one of them on their own is the whole story, more likely that they all play a part to a greater or lesser extent.

There are, however, three possible explanations I think we can dismiss at the outset.

The Label

Some people feel that the word "only" is partly to blame for the generally negative aura surrounding children without siblings. In the English language the word is often used to indicate a lack of something desirable as in "He's only got one pair of shoes." Indeed, it is hard to ask a parent whether they have any more children without sounding disparaging: "Is she your only one?" So people have suggested that if we changed the label for example to "single child" these negative connotations would drop off.

That seems unlikely. First of all, negative stereotypes of only children exist in countries where the words used to describe them carries no unfortunate associations. The French phrase *enfant unique* has, if anything, a positive ring to it, in that *unique* means both "sole/only" and "unrivalled/unparalleled". Yet *enfants uniques* have as bad a reputation in France as only children have in English language countries such as Britain and the USA.

Second, "only" is not necessarily a negative term, even in English. When lovers say to each other, "You are my only love," it is intended as a compliment. And when the Gospels proclaimed Jesus Christ as "the only begotten son of God the Father", they were referring to His uniqueness, not His Father's infertility problems. The label is irrelevant. It is what is believed to be in the package that counts.

Early Research

We saw earlier that some poorly conducted research studies from the turn of the century came up with very negative findings about only children. It has been suggested that they had an important influence in shaping popular opinion about the effects of growing up without siblings. However, while they doubtless contributed to the myth, they cannot have started it, since the very first study of all, by Bohannon, shows that the teachers he questioned already believed only children to be maladjusted. And the fact that these negative findings received such wide circulation, and retained their hold even in the face of other, more positive findings, suggests they struck a chord with myths which were already in circulation.

Only Children in Fiction

One ingenious explanation put forward by Ellen Peck, author of a US book on only children, is that the myths are just that – they have arisen as a result of people reading stories in which only children are portrayed in a bad light. That seems at first sight to be plausible. The maladjusted, pampered, lonely wimp is a stock character in both adult and children's fiction, going back at least to Zola's *Fécondité* (1899). The "spoilt brat" also has a long history of which the juiciest example ever is Richmal Crompton's Violet Elizabeth Bott, who could memorably "Thcream n' thcream till I'm thick." These stereotyped, pampered only children are often contrasted with and redeemed by an impoverished but jolly large family. In the 1940s and 1950s this was one of Noel Streatfield's favourite themes. Lalla in *White Boots* and Millie in *The Children of Primrose Lane* are both conceited and pushy only children who are rightly taken down a peg in the course of the story. Yet, they are likeable as well as awful; partly because it is made clear that their behaviour derives from their particular upbringing and partly because they are also shown as resourceful and imaginative children who spur the plot along.

And that is where the explanation breaks down. For the only child wimps and brats are greatly outnumbered in fiction by only child heroes and heroines. The "only" orphan is a stock character (Oliver Twist, Pip in *Great Expectations*, Jane Eyre, Heidi, Anne of Green Gables), but even main characters with a full complement of parents are often sibling-free. Inspector Morse is an only child, as are P. D. James' two detectives, Adam Dalgleish and Cordelia Gray. Roald Dahl, Jane Gardham, Penelope Lively, Helen Cresswell and Anne Pillen all frequently cast only children as heroes or heroines in their novels and children's books. As such, they are portrayed as intelligent, courageous, humorous and concerned for others – a positive advertisement for the one-child family.

I am not suggesting that these authors intentionally set out to show only children in a good light – it is probably just more convenient to have a leading character who is unencumbered with sibling complications. But the net effect is to provide a whole range of positive images of only children, which quite outweigh the occasional negative reference. If anything, fiction presents a quite unrealistically positive stereotype. Since only children tend to be great readers, that may conceivably help to explain why, despite their consciousness of negative stereotypes, most still retain good self-esteem.

The three explanations above seem rather unlikely. However, there are a number of other ideas as to how myths about only children arose and persist, which do fit in better with historical fact and psychological and sociological theories.

Stepping Out of Line

All human societies develop customs, traditions and standards of behaviour to which most people conform. These norms help society to run smoothly and are therefore an essential part of its functioning. As members of society we quickly learn to respond to pressures to act "normally". We feel secure when we act according to custom and we feel threatened when other people do not, because that calls into question our own behaviour.

Historically, the norm has been for parents to have large families. That was partly a result of basic biology; as long as a couple had a sexual relationship and no access to contraception, babies would arrive at regular intervals. But it was also a result of enlightened self-interest. In farming communities, where most people lived, many hands made lighter work. Hence, a value was placed on quantity of children – "a full quiver" to till the fields, milk the cows and support you in old age.

Of course, some parents even then had only one child, through secondary infertility, loss of one or both parents, or the death of other children. That will have presented no threat to traditional values – it happened through misfortune and the parents could be pitied, a very comfortable emotion. The real challenge came at the end of the 19th century with increasing urbanisation and access to contraception. Some parents began choosing to have only one child, preferring to use limited resources to opt for quality rather than quantity. That decision challenged the value of the large family and threatened to undermine the belief that many children were a blessing. Small wonder if in those circumstances, one-child families – both parents and children – began to be looked on with disfavour.

The Road to Extinction

Another linked explanation is that one-child families challenge the basic instinct of every living thing to preserve and increase its own species or group by reproduction. Historically, large families served a useful purpose in maintaining the number of people a community or nation needed for it to defend itself against outsiders and preserve its traditions. Small families do less to build up numbers, but one-child families are a real threat to them. Theoretically, if every couple in a community had only one child, it would lead to extinction, but even if the one-child family merely became a popular choice, it could lead to a dramatic reduction in the size of the group, leaving it vulnerable to attack or outside influence. It may be, as Toni Falbo says, that "It is to the group's advantage to promote belief in the only child stereotype, because such beliefs implicitly encourage parents to have at least two children" and thereby keep numbers up.

The prospect of a declining population created real concern in many Western countries in the late 19th and early 20th centuries, at a time when the environmental costs of population growth were not appreciated and when it was seen rather as the key to economic, political and military power. It seems possible that the one-child family was perceived as a threat to national interests and that people and politicians instinctively or consciously reacted against it – extolling the virtues of the large family and denigrating the small. In 1904 the Royal Commission on the Decline of the Birth Rate in New South Wales declared that "The life of an only child is an uninterrupted lesson in egoism lasting 20 years ... the benefits of large families to the members of those families and to the nation composed of them cannot be overestimated."

Western anxiety about the effects of falling birth rates continued and grew more intense during the 1920s and 1930s when one-child families became quite common. In Britain, respected academics like Richard Titmuss made dire predictions about "the extinction of the white race". Totalitarian governments in the USSR, Germany and Italy explicitly promoted large families in the 1930s, and, in a less extreme fashion other countries tried to do the same. The defeat of France in the Second World War was partly attributed to the decline in its population and between 1945 and 1955 governments made efforts to increase the numbers of larger families in order to revitalise the country. A French sociologist, Jean-Pierre Almodovar, suggests that this accounts for the gradual appearance over that period of many very negative pronouncements about only children by French child-care experts – they were politically motivated by a desire to deter parents from having only one child, which was seen as contrary to the interests of the state. It also seems possible that, at a less conscious level, falling birth rates give rise to a collective panic in which myths about only children can flourish. In similar climates of panic, myths have arisen around other minority groups – Jews, blacks, and more recently, single mothers.

A Change in Only Children

So far we have assumed that the myths have been fabrications designed to serve national and social interests. However, it does seem possible that the only children of the 20th century, on whom the research is based, are different from those in earlier times. Historically, children whose lack of siblings arose through misadventure may well have come from family situations which predisposed them to unhappiness and psychological problems. Because they were exceptional, their behaviour will have stood out, and helped form the stereotype.

In contrast, many only children in the first half of the 20th century will have lacked siblings through parental choice. Equipped with a full complement of parents, and devoid of any tragic complications, they were as well equipped as any other child to benefit from growing up in a small family. By the time family size rose again, and only children once more arose largely through necessity, the only-child stereotype was in circulation. Since no one wants their child to be thought spoiled or lonely, parents may have made special efforts to guard against it, thus producing the marginally better adjusted children identified in many research studies.

The three linked explanations considered above (undermining of norms, fears about population decline, and changes in only children over the century) seem to fit both history and geography. Though it is not possible to tell when and where negative attitudes to only children arose, they seem to have become noticeable around the late 19th century in countries such as Britain, the USA, Australia and France, where contraception was becoming both widely available and socially acceptable and where the birth rate was falling. They do not seem to have arisen in countries such as Italy, Spain and Portugal, where, until very recently, contraception and abortion were frowned on or even outlawed, family sizes were still large in accordance with traditional norms and the birth rate remained relatively high. (In the past two decades of course, the absence of a stereotype in these countries has meant that with contraception now widely available, the proportion of couples choosing to have an only child has rocketed. Will similar myths take root there too?)

Plausible as these explanations are, however, I don't think they are the whole story. We still have to account for the remarkable fact that although people may have been inclined to believe only children are doomed, they must have noticed that most in fact turn out fine. To explain this discrepancy we have to turn from sociology to individual psychology.

Sweeping Statements and Selective Perception

We are all born theoreticians. We come ready programmed to make generalisations from the specific experiences we encounter. Faced with a range of furry, four-legged creatures of all shapes, sizes and colours, a toddler quickly classifies them all as "doggies". The ability to make generalisations is an essential part of human functioning – it helps us make sense of the world, predict events and plan action. But it can lead us astray. The trouble is that once we have made our general classification, we tend to ignore information that does not fit in. The dog-knowledgeable toddler encountering a cat for the first time will again say "doggie" despite the fact that it mews instead of barks. For centuries, sailors believed the world was flat because the sea they were on looked flat, despite the hundreds of ships they must have seen appearing over the horizon mast first. We overgeneralise from our limited experience – we make sweeping statements. We only see the things that fit our theory – we operate "selective perception".

These very normal processes may help to explain why so many "experts" have got it so wrong in relation to only children. As we saw earlier, psychiatrists, therapists and paediatricians have been very influential in promoting the only-child myth. One reason may be that, by virtue of their work, they spend much of their time with people who have problems. Like the rest of us, they face the temptation to generalise from the people they meet to the rest of the population – hence they may come to believe that every little girl harbours incestuous fantasies about her father or that every child who is separated from his or her mother in early life will develop problems later on.

The experts meet both sibling children and only children, since both are equally likely to have problems, and they face some temptation to generalise in either case. However, when it comes to sibling children, the temptation is reduced by the fact that the experts have a "normal" group of sibling children as a comparison. Most people they meet socially will have siblings, so will most of their family, so in all likelihood will they, and they are also very likely to have more than one child themselves. So it is obvious to them that not all sibling children have problems. But when it comes to only children, the temptation is greater. Since only children are thin on the ground, the experts have no "normal" group to act as a reference point and to provide examples who are well adjusted. So it is fatally easy first of all to attribute the patient's problems to the fact that they are the only child in the family. They are attention-seeking and egocentric? They lack friends? It's the "only-child syndrome". From there it is but a step to generalise their clinical experience to all only children and produce sweeping statements that "only children tend to be attention-seeking, egocentric and without friends".

A good example is provided by Stephanie Siegel's book on adopted children, which we looked at in Chapter 6. Dr Siegel is a therapist whose experience is in counselling adoptive families who have problems. She also has three adopted children herself. Her book is addressed to all adoptive families and she prefaces it by saying that though it is based on her clinical experience. "Incidents you read about in these pages may be very like your own experience ... because *all adoptive families have a great deal in common*".

My italics underline Dr Siegel's assumption that the families she encounters who have problems are like those she has never met who do not. That is a doubtful supposition, but, in the case of adopted children with siblings, it is probably modified by experience of her own family. However, when it comes to adopted only children, her main experience is of those in therapy. So she takes it for granted that the problems they have are likely to be found in all adopted only children and pronounces accordingly.

It is not surprising that "experts" have sometimes got it wrong. But it is worrying when their inaccurate and invalid generalisations are treated as gospel. Nor does it stop there. Not content with lumbering all only children with the reputation of the minority who have problems, they sometimes go on to pile on top of that the bad behaviour of sibling children, who are acting in a way that is supposedly typical of the only child.

An early example of this in action comes from Brill's book *Psychoanalysis – its theories and practical applications*, published in 1922. Brill discusses only children in conjunction with "favourite children" who have siblings, which is fair enough, except that he keeps ascribing the faults of the latter to the former. For example, in one paragraph he starts off by claiming that

> It is due to the undivided attention and abnormal love that the only child gets from his parents that he develops into a confirmed egotist … It is therefore no wonder that [he] becomes vain and one-sided … begrudges the happiness of friends and acquaintances and is therefore shunned and disliked.

However, the two case studies Brill uses to demonstrate this point are both of favourite children with siblings – a son who suffered from severe depression and envy when his friends were successful in the money market, and "Joseph of the Bible" whose boasting led to rejection by his brothers.

This quite unconscious dodge of establishing that only children are maladjusted by referring to the behaviour problems of children with siblings is not confined to experts. I have also noticed it in discussions with colleagues and friends. One acquaintance who started off frankly declaring "I can't stand only children" continued to tell me that what really got up her nose was their attention-seeking behaviour. As an illustration she then recounted a long story of a family in which the adults could never have a proper conversation because they were constantly interrupted by the children. I wasn't sure that I heard her correctly.

"How many children do they have?"
"Three."

You might suppose that people who live and work among a more representative group of only children would be less prone to stereotype them, since they must encounter plenty who are just like anyone else. (And indeed one study does suggest that teachers have more positive attitudes than other people.) The trouble is that, once established, prejudice of any kind is self-reinforcing. When we meet someone who fits the stereotype, they confirm it and stick in our minds. When we meet someone who does not, we forget about them or treat them as an exception. "She's so outgoing and confident" a nursery-school teacher said of my four-year-old. "You'd never think she was an only child." We chalk up the bad behaviour and discount the good. "He's a very difficult little boy" an elderly great aunt observed after a trying visit, "An only child of course." A few months later after a more successful stay she was full of admiration. "Such a bright and lively lad!" No mention of lack of siblings on that occasion. And of course, attributing disturbed behaviour to only-child status is part of the self-perpetuation of the myth. When a child (or adult) from a larger family is peculiar or obnoxious, people produce a variety of explanations, of which the most usual is the way they have been brought up. When an only child behaves in the same way, they look no further than family size. There are probably just enough only children who fit the stereotype in some respect to keep the myth ticking over.

But the most insidious aspect of any sort of stereotype is that it becomes so much part of our thinking that we are quite unconscious of it – we have "internalised" it. We are all now aware of the dangers of this in relation to race and gender, perhaps to an exaggerated extent, but we have yet to become conscious of it in relation to only children. The result is that even when people try to be even-handed, they find themselves slipping into bias. The very first article I wrote on only children was published in a magazine concerned with children's issues. They were eager to take it, printed it as written, did not quibble at all at the message that only children are no more likely to be lonely, spoiled and maladjusted than anyone else. But they headed it with a half-page photograph of a rather sad little girl, totally alone in an empty church, on her knees in prayer (for a baby brother no doubt). A graphic contradiction of everything I was saying.

Believing the Worst about Yourself

Bias in expert opinion and in media presentation may account to some extent for the perpetuation of myths about only children. But what about the testimony of those concerned? If the stereotype is without foundation, why do only children themselves confirm it? Why do so many say themselves that they were unhappy, lonely, spoiled and overprotected, that, as a consequence, they have problems in relating to other people and, at the very least, that they regret not having brothers and sisters?

There are a number of possible reasons. One is that there are, of course, only children who have had poor experiences and been damaged as a result. The research does not tell us that the one-child family is a perfect place for children – it has its failures. What it tells us is that it is as good a place as any other, and that the majority of children emerge from it as happy, well-adjusted adults. But because bad news is good news while good news is no news, we tend to hear the complaints of the minority who had problems rather than the plaudits of the majority who did not.

However, another likely explanation is that, as we know from other forms of prejudice, those who are the butt of it can come to believe in it themselves. Black children can feel they *are* inferior, girls that they *are* hopeless at science and only children that they are indeed lonely or spoiled or maladjusted and that they have missed something vital in not having a sibling. There is evidence that children as young as nine are well aware of the stereotype and that they often subscribe to it themselves, perhaps not surprising when an approved infant reading scheme contains such a gem as "Once upon a time, a little prince lived in a palace in a far off country. His name was Paul. He had no brothers or sisters and he was very lonely."

And finally, it has to be said that some only children are all too happy to ascribe any problems they may have to the fact that they lacked siblings. It is the perfect peg to hang their difficulties on. It also conveniently absolves them from responsibility for them. If they have a failed marriage, poor social relationsips or trouble in holding down a job, it is not because of their own personal deficiencies, but because their parents failed to provide them with the essential experience of brothers and sisters.

The Sibling Myth

For the only-child myths would lose much of their force if it were not for the corresponding myths about siblings. The belief that the large family is the happiest and healthiest family runs deep. Brothers and sisters having fun together, supporting each other in times of stress, learning to share and cooperate; that is the ideal to which most parents aim. The more the merrier – the Waltons, the Gilbreths in *Cheaper by the Dozen*, the large Victorian families of *What Katy Did*, *Little Women* and the books of E. Nesbit. Even though the ideal family size is now down to two, that number is still reckoned to provide the minimum basic ingredients for a happy childhood – fun, companionship, support and the "rough and tumble" needed for the development of a healthy personality.

In fact, as many sibling children are well aware, the idyllic sibling childhood is a myth, and one whose credibility has been seriously dented by recent research. The reality, as revealed by researchers such as Judy Dunn, is that relationships between brothers and sisters vary enormously, from the very affectionate to the hostile and aggressive. Some siblings are a great comfort to each other; others a continual irritation. There is evidence that they tend to resolve differences as they get older, but, at the time, living with a sibling is not unalloyed bliss – even those who are basically very fond of each other can spend a lot of time needling, teasing and reducing each other to tears. And while the birth of a younger child can be a great excitement and a positive developmental experience for the older one, it often causes temporary distress and occasionally creates lasting damage. Siblings may or may not hit it off, and while parents can do a great deal to help them get on well, much depends on whether the basic temperaments they are born with clash or complement each other. Having a sibling is a bit of a gamble, and, as research on only children has shown, it is no developmental advantage.

So how has the sibling myth evolved? As we have seen, there are probably good sociological reasons for it. Large families help foster a growing population and even two-child families will maintain it. The idea that children are happier and healthier with siblings helps to reassure parents that the hard work involved is worth it, and a belief that quarrels and tears are an essential part of learning to get on with others allows both parents and children to see them in a more positive light.

One-child families present a significant threat to the sibling myth, particularly if parents have chosen to have one child, seem happy with their choice and have a child who is flourishing. "If it's that easy", parents of larger families may feel, "have we gone to all that trouble for nothing?" The uncomfortable feeling that you may have made the wrong choice is a phenomenon psychologists call "cognitive dissonance", and they believe we extricate ourselves from it by reinterpreting the situation so that it once again appears to justify our efforts. Thus the idea evolves that only children must be disadvantaged in some other, less obvious way. They have more possessions, so that will make them "spoiled". They don't have to share, so that makes them selfish. They avoid conflicts with siblings, so they must be lonely. They get more time and attention than sibling children, so that is redefined as "overattention" and claimed to be bad for them. Add the lot together and you have maladjustment. Such ideas are certainly sometimes retailed to children in larger families to allay any envy of only children. Presumably that also contributes to the stereotype.

So here we have two myths, neither of which matches reality, both of which reinforce each other. The positive stereotype of the sibling child and the negative stereotype of the only child are two sides of the same coin. If having siblings makes children happy and well adjusted, only children cannot be like that. If being an only child makes you lonely and spoiled, it has been worth the effort of having more than one.

The dual myth has some very positive spin-offs for larger families. It bolsters their self-esteem, reassures them that they have made the right choice and allows them to ride out the rough passages with confidence. However, it can have very negative effects on some families with an only child. It can undermine the parents' confidence in their choice or aggravate their sadness at their fate. It can cause great anxiety about how their child will turn out and can lead them to misinterpret perfectly normal childhood behaviour as the pathological result of lack of sibling company. It tells the child that they are deprived in some essential way, encourages them to view their experience as defective, and, of course, allows them to shift the blame for their problems onto their parents.

An interesting example of the two myths in operation comes from the bestselling advice book, *Families and How to Survive Them* by Robin Skynner, a family therapist and the oldest of five children, and John Cleese, an ex-patient and an only child. The book consists of a written conversation between them. In a chapter entitled "Healthier by the Dozen", they compare their childhood experiences to give the basic message "many children, good; one child, bad". But the conversation is striking for the discrepancy between their described experiences and the conclusions they draw from them.

Robin Skynner says:
    I was the eldest of five boys. And I certainly do remember it. There's
    a feeling of sunshine and bliss in connection with the first four years,

until the brother next to me arrived and then it's as if a bomb went off and after that, for a long time the general feeling is grey and dismal. Like many eldest children, I'm sure I was spoiled at first, then resented the new arrival even more because of that and got myself in everyone's bad books as a result. I also think my family had a fear of jealousy over several generations so my parents had it behind the screen. Therefore, they tried to stop me being jealous by giving in to me, when they would have done more good by drawing firm lines within which I could learn to cope and gradually get over it ... Jealous squabbles were always breaking out between us and our parents could never find a way of handling it successfully. "We can't understand why they're all so jealous" they'd say to people, "We try to be fair."

John Cleese says:

I was an only child and I can see that I missed out on a lot of the lessons you learn from having to deal with the natural rivalry with both brothers and sisters. So I'm sure I had competitiveness and envy behind the screen to some extent and it was only when I came into your group that I began to see it more clearly. [*R.S.: What else do you think you missed as an "only"?*] Oh the rough and tumble. I was more fragile than my friends ... Then again because you're the only one, I think you get the idea that you are a bit "special". Perhaps that's why I find that I share some of the "outsider" attitudes you've described. Any finally, because your parents have only you, it's harder to escape and become independent of them.

These accounts are remarkable, not just because, as they stand, they are hardly an advertisement for the large family (Robin Skynner was clearly happier before all those siblings came along – and note the way the very real emotional pain of childhood conflict is transformed via the cosy phrase "rough and tumble" into something an only child can feel they have "missed out" on) but because of the double standard the authors are operating. Robin Skynner's experience was damaging, not because large families are intrinsically prone to jealousy and squabbles, but because his parents mishandled things – first, "spoiling" him, then failing to deal effectively with his resentment and jealousy. John Cleese's experiences were damaging, not because of the way his parents handled things, but because being an only child intrinsically leaves you prone to concealed jealousy, fragility, dependency and feelings of being an outsider. The authors *particularise* the sibling experience, explaining away the negatives as due to mishandling. They *generalise* the only child experience, accentuating the negatives as inevitable consequences of lack of siblings. Being an only child may be all right at the time, but it is bad for you.

Now that is nonsense. Some individual only children may indeed have problems that are due to the particular kind of only childhood they had (and John Cleese's experience does seem to have been particularly sheltered, isolated and peripatetic). But as a general explanation of adult problems, "I'm an only child" will not do. If, as is claimed here, an only childhood, with its lack of jealousy, its close relationships and feelings of being special, inevitably led to problems, that would show up in large-scale studies comparing the personal adjustment of only and sibling children. It does not. The conclusion has to be that only children's adult problems are due not to their having been an only child *as such*, which is the claim made in the book, but to the particular kind of only childhood they had, along with other important factors such as the temperament they inherited from their parents and the experiences they encountered while growing up.

The reality seems to be that being an only child and having brothers and sisters both have their pros and cons and both are equally good for children. But, because of the myths, we tend to accentuate the negatives of being an only child and ignore the positives. With sibling children it is the other way around. When only children say they want a brother or sister we take that as evidence that they feel fundamentally deprived and unhappy with their lot. When sibling children say they hate their brother or sister and wish they were an only child, we brush that off as a childish phase. "They don't really mean it." They can't do. Having a sibling is fun. And that's an order!

Do the Myths Matter?

It seems clear that, for a variety of reasons, myths about only children and about siblings are widespread, and that many only children believe in them. Stereotyping of other groups has been attacked and outlawed from civilised society – should we add "onlyism" to racism and sexism, start banning negative portrayals of only children from the library shelves and organise consciousness-raising sessions for depressed adult "onlies"?

I am not sure that would be helpful. Only children are not a disadvantaged group who suffer from poor self-esteem, nor are they discriminated against in the workplace. They do pretty well already, and the last thing they need is an insurgence of triumphalism, which would play right into the hands of the myth-monger. Some of the not-too-serious self-stereotyping lends a becoming modesty to otherwise successful careers. "Of course, I'm one of those screwed-up only children" they say as they sail to the top. It may even be the case that the stereotype has had a useful function in alerting parents to the possibility of overindulgence, selfishness and loneliness and that part of the reason contemporary only children do not conform to the stereotype is that their parents have made damned sure they do not.

What is far more important than adding a new dimension to "political correctness" is to ensure that the very reassuring research findings on only children are widely known. In particular, those who are seen as "experts" (psychiatrists, psychologists, paediatricians, therapists and counsellors) and those who set themselves up as reliable informers (the press, television and radio, authors of advice books) should get their facts straight and present them without bias. The myths cause quite needless anxiety to many parents and there is no excuse for professionals and the media increasing that anxiety by reinforcing them. The best outcome as far as I am concerned would be if only children and their parents could continue to laugh at themselves while not believing a word of the current myths.

CHAPTER NINE

Some Ingredients for a Happy Only Childhood

I start this chapter with some misgivings. Despite much research on the subject, no one really knows the best way to bring up children and we know even less about bringing up only children, since on that topic there is no research at all. Furthermore, my encounters with only children and their parents have convinced me that there is no one right way to rear an only child. For the interviews revealed what the statistical research tends to conceal – the astonishing variety of one-child families. What I saw in my interviews were parents bringing up their children in very different ways, in accordance with their own particular values, person-alities and cultural milieux. Some were closely protective of their children, others encouraged them to early independence. Some were permissive, others fairly authoritarian. Some kept open house, others preferred a cosy threesome. They had much more in common with other parents from similar social backgrounds than they did with each other.

Finally, I am nervous about rocking the boat. "If it ain't broke, don't fix it" goes the saying. Judging by research results, most parents of only children are already doing a good job. Why offer them gratuitous advice which might be counterproductive?

Well, one reason is that not everyone gets it right. There are a minority of only children who are indeed lonely, spoiled, overprotected and unhappy, and who later in life bitterly regret not having had siblings. It seems that their parents could have benefited from hearing what other parents of happier only children have done. Because one-child families are thin on the ground, parents do not get the chance to exchange experiences informally in the way that those with larger families do. And most cannot draw on their own childhood experiences, since they are not only children themselves.

Another reason is that though in most respects bringing up only children is like bringing up any other child, there do seem to be a few specific challenges which one-child parents have to meet. All children have to be kept from investigating light sockets; to be nagged to do their homework; to be sympathised with when their best friend deserts them. But only one-child parents have to explain to their children why everyone else in the class has a brother or sister; to plan for who their child is going to play with while they are on holiday; to keep them company on a rainy Sunday when all their friends are away. Many of them have worked at successful strategies for dealing with these challenges and, though there is no evidence for it, I suspect that those strategies may possibly make the difference between a childhood that merely turns out a reasonably happy, well-adjusted adult and one that is looked back on with pleasure and no regrets.

This chapter therefore simply passes on to parents (or prospective parents) of any only child, some of the things that have worked for others. It is based partly on advice collected from 168 US one-child parents by Sharryl Hawke and David Knox, partly on the experiences and views of the only children and their parents I interviewed, and partly on my own experience as an only child and as the mother of two "only" children. Many of the ideas in it are confirmed by another small study of one-child parents recently carried out by Beryl Riley at the University of East Anglia. It is not comprehensive, nor is it authoritative. Nor, since no one has studied parenting in a representative group of one-child families, is it necessarily typical of all parents of only children. It is simply a list of suggestions. If you find them helpful, or if they give you other ideas to try, well and good. If they don't fit your situation, or if they seem to you nonsense, ignore them. Try something else, watch the results and act accordingly. Parents are all, perforce, experimentalists. Above all, please remember that when I say "It is a good idea to ...", "It's important to ..." or even "Don't ..." it is only my opinion. The whole of this chapter is opinion. Feel free to disagree.

Dealing with your own Feelings

You may have an only child by choice, in which case you are likely to feel positive about it, which is good for you and for your child. But if you have very much wanted more children and have had to settle for one through circumstances, you may be left with feelings of great unhappiness at the blow fate has dealt you, or resentment at the partner who has pressured you into stopping at one. It is important that you try to deal with those feelings, because if you don't you risk passing them on to your child. Many only children are acutely aware of their parents' moods and attitudes, and if you feel sad or resentful about them being the only one, they may well end up feeling the same way.

People deal with unhappiness in different ways. Acknowledging it to yourself, talking it over with someone you are close to or to a trained counsellor are the best ways for many people, but others prefer just to put it behind them and deliberately make a fresh start. Whatever you do, it may help to remember that you are being sad for yourself – you wanted another child and are not able have one. You do not have to be sad for your child. They are just as likely to turn out happy and well adjusted as they would have been with siblings. Whether they are so depends on your providing a positive atmosphere for them to grow up in.

Creating a Good Relationship with your Child

Good parent–child relationships are important for any child. But they may be particularly important for only children. If sibling children are rejected, abused or even just temporarily at loggerheads with their parents, they may be able to turn to their brother or sister for comfort and support. Within the family, an only child just has you. It is therefore vital that you get it right.

Only children do not seem necessarily closer to their parents, but I suspect that a slightly different kind of relationship may develop with them because their parents have to take on some of the role that siblings would play in larger families. Part of that is having someone to confide in and part of it is providing, at least some of the time, a companion of equal status. The two interconnect, as this father points out.

Even with brothers and sisters that don't talk very well if there's a problem, there's always somebody there that they can turn to. Whether it be bullying in the playground or anything. There's somebody there they can use as an ally or a weapon. Whereas Chrissie is so totally on her own that we maybe have got to come down a wee bit from a parent–child scenario to a kind of friendship, and although we're your parents we're still your flesh and blood, so tell us anything that goes wrong. You have more of a friendly relationship with one child because you get to know them from being with them and being around them. Now she's quite good company and it's very encouraging. A pal, you know.

Some parents find being a companion to their child easier than others. If you really like children and have a lot of energy, you will probably enjoy it thoroughly. If you are basically more interested in adult life and are older than average, you may have to make more of an effort. One father who was himself an only child said:

I think that the relationship I want to have with Luke, doing a lot of things with him, is a very conscious reversal of the relationship I had with my father. I don't recall my father doing much with us because by the time I was of an age he was in his late fifties and I was always very embarrassed about that. I remember a dreadful occasion on the beach – my father sneezed and his false teeth fell out! I just wanted the earth to swallow me! I don't think he ever kicked a ball with me. But Luke and I have from an early age, three or four, gone away together, youth hostelling, camping, mountain biking, skiing. I think it's also partly a conscious strategy that I would like us both to be close to him and that he would be be able to talk to us, and we were just saying the other day, that it's an interesting contrast that compared with all his pals, he is a lot more open with us than his friends are with their families. [*How do you know that?*] Well, just because of listening to conversation with other parents. He will tell us things, not just about other friends but about what he does. I have I think always quite explicitly said to him that we would like him to be able to tell us and expect him to tell us if he does things that are – unusual, and I have always taken the line that I will never blame you the first time you do something, but would want to know what you are doing in order to let you know if it is right or wrong.

As we saw in Chapter 4, there are different ways of being a companion to your child. You can help them get involved in your adult pursuits by making them interesting to a child, and that is worth doing, even if, to start with, letting them have a go at a simple job takes ten times as long as it would you on your own. As they acquire more skill and experience, they will eventually be a genuine partner in the enterprise. Alternatively, you can join in their interests and have fun with them at their level. Either way, you are giving your child a rich experience that they will look back on with pleasure for the rest of their lives.

Creating this kind of warm, involved and fairly egalitarian parental relationship is important for only children because three is an awkward number. If the parents remain on their pedestal, making all the decisions and issuing orders, the child can feel consistently outgunned. If the parents are always involved with each other and with adult pursuits, their child can feel very left out. "The children of lovers are orphans," wrote Robert Louis Stevenson, himself an only child. It's a happier situation if the child can sometimes pair off with one parent and sometimes be part of an equal threesome as in these two families.

We're really happy doing things with Lorraine [four-year-old]. In fact she calls us the Three Musketeers. "All for one and one for all". Honestly, we're very happy just the three of us.

He's got Bill's sense of humour, Bill's sense of fun and I like to sort of react to it. Something happened last week. I am the world's most enthusiastic shopper and I've never had a Visa card you see, but because we're going to America we decided that I had better get a Visa card. So the card came through and we'd been to the pictures the night before to see the film *Cop and a Half* about this precocious American child. One of the lines in it is that he becomes a policeman and it's your worst nightmare: a ten-year-old with a badge. When I got this Visa card out, Bill said "Well, that's it!" and Lawrence said "That's your worst nightmare: a forty-year-old with a credit card!" I thought this is it! There's two of them at me now! If we go into town and go shopping, outside Marks and Spencers, he'll stand and go "No, Mum! Don't go in! Don't buy!" Right in the middle of the street! So that's the kind of thing.

Now, this sort of egalitarian relationship, being a friend to your child, is something that some "experts" warn one-child parents against. They suggest that it will create confusion because the "boundary" between adult and child will become blurred – the parents will have trouble in asserting authority when that is necessary, and the child will feel insecure, because the parents are not clearly in charge.

That seems to me to underestimate both parents and children. Parents can be fun one moment and strict the next, and in my experience most children have no difficulty whatsoever in recognising which is which and acting accordingly. In suggesting that friendly, confiding, egalitarian relationships are good for only children, I do not mean that they should happen all the time. Obviously, there are many decisions that parents are responsible for making, and when only children step out of line, they have to be shown in no uncertain terms that such behaviour is unacceptable. But that aspect of the parental role is not incompatible with being a trusted companion. It just means that parents have to balance the two.

Because good parent–child relationships are so important to only children, if things go wrong, I think you should get worried. No set of parents and children get on well all the time, and every family has its rough patches, but if the negatives in your relationship outweigh the positives over a period of months, try to do something about it. Think about where it all started and what might have set things off. Talk *with* your child – listen to how they see things and explain to them how you see things. See if between you, you can find a way of getting on better together. If that does not work, consider getting outside help.

Encouraging Independence

Close relationships with their parents are good for only children, but so is independence from them. There are two sides to that – you have to encourage your child to be independent of you and you have to ensure that you are not dependent on them.

Most children have a strong drive towards independence. "I can do it *myself*!" Capitalising on that by letting them try, while keeping an eye on safety, gives them increased confidence and encourages them to further independence. Hovering over them and protecting them from every eventuality convinces them that the world away from you is indeed a dangerous place. If you encourage your child to venture out in ways appropriate to their age (from weekends with Granny to two months' Inter-railing) you will give them confidence that the outside world is a good place. And you will let them feel that they have a life of their own, separate from yours, which balances the bits of your life which are separate from them.

For it is equally important for parents to be independent of their children, and parents of an only child may have to take extra care to be so, particularly in later life. Feeling you are the one thing that gives meaning to your parents' life is a heavy burden for an only child to carry. You are probably less likely to land them in that position if you try to ensure from the start that you have a life of your own. Don't give up everything to devote yourself to your child, or you are likely to make them feel very guilty later on. Keep up your own interests, your own friendships and your work if that is possible. When your child leaves home, make sure you build up an independent and satisfying life of your own so that they can enjoy visiting you, rather than feel they have to. Work out with your partner what you are going to do if either or both of you become unable to look after yourselves and try to arrange your affairs so that you are not financially dependent on your child in old age.

One of the mothers I spoke to, who was an only child herself, had consciously been trying to avoid being dependent on her own son in the way her mother was with her:

> I would like to think that what we were doing was allowing Christopher to be independent and to do things that he wanted to do and not to be feeling guilty, because I think that's what I feel a lot of the time. I would not want him, as an only child, to be in the position where he felt that he was totally responsible for our happiness or whatever. I think, even just looking at him, that he is quite a confident little boy. He can go away with friends and we can go away for a week somewhere. That is good for us and for him.

An ideal scenario for an only child is if they have a close relationship with their parents from which each of them can venture out into independent lives of their own. The same mother said:

> The interesting thing is I think we're doing something that most of our friends are not at the moment. Because we do only have one child, we actually have a lot of time when we're together, because he's doing something else. Whereas people we know who have more than one child have got somebody around all the time. If Christopher is off for the weekend or the day, we have the time together and we will go off and do things together during the day or go out somewhere in the evening together and don't need a babysitter so we can just go. I think we probably spend a lot more time, just the two of us than a lot of other families.

Avoiding Overindulgence

When you have only one child, you have more time to spend with them. That is good for children and you should not stint it. You also have more money to spend on them, and that, many one-child parents feel, you should watch. Most parents want their children to learn the value of money and to develop the ability to wait for things, and that is hampered if they always get what they want right away.

What is more, money can divide children. If your child is the only one in the class with a video recorder in their bedroom, five pounds' pocket money and a new outfit every week, it is likely to set up problems of envy and resentment. For those reasons, many one-child parents try to limit their child to what seems to be the norm for their circle of friends. Some indeed overdo it. One great advantage of having a lot of contact with other families with young children is that it gives you a realistic baseline of what is the going rate.

You may have problems in keeping possessions within bounds if your child, as well as being your only one, is also the only grandchild (or the only one of present-receiving age). It is fun for grandparents to buy things for their grandchildren, and in practice it can be quite difficult to stop them overdoing it without offending them. But it is worth trying – perhaps by suggesting they limit presents to one on special occasions like birthdays and Christmas or that they make some of the presents things that the child would get anyway, like clothes or books or sports equipment, rather than a box of chocolates or a new soft toy every Sunday.

No child should be overindulged in the sense of getting away with bad behaviour, and only children are in as much need of firmness and limit-setting as any other. Acting as a "pal" to your child and having fun with them does not preclude being the authority figure when that is necessary, and your child should know that the fun and games only operate while they are behaving well. Don't be afraid to switch to authority mode when other children are around if your child is not acting appropriately with them or with you. If that leads to a set-to, you needn't feel too mortified that your child has shown their worst side publicly – remember that sibling children are well used to seeing their brothers and sisters in screaming rages or floods of tears and think none the worse of them.

Finally, if your child shows a tendency to put on the pounds, watch it. The reasons why some only children are more likely to become overweight are not fully understood, but circumstantial evidence suggests it may be to do with diet and lack of exercise. Keep sweets, sweet biscuits, cakes and junk food for treats and, if you can, discourage relatives from giving them as presents. Don't pressure your child into eating adult-sized portions.

See that they get some form of regular exercise. Let them try out various sports and see if they enjoy them, but if, as some only children seem to be, they are non-competitive by nature, find other activities instead. Swimming is excellent exercise, and so is the deeply unfashionable activity of walking to and from school. You could also encourage your child to cycle or walk to clubs and friends' houses rather than driving them everywhere in the car. Of course, you have to teach them how to do so safely and supervise them too, at least in the early stages.

Keeping your Expectations Realistic

Most one-child parents do not seem to have unrealistic expectations for their children, but a few undoubtedly do. Expectations are not necessarily a bad thing – they can help a child to try things and thus to have a sense of achievement. The trick is to balance them so that they help the child along without making them feel uncomfortably under pressure.

Only children at the pre-school age can give a misleading impression of being older than their years. Because they spend so much time with adults, their language and some of their behaviour can seem surprisingly mature. But they are still pre-schoolers, not grown-ups, so do not be disappointed if they lapse from time to time. Try not to rush to the conclusion that "immature" behaviour is a sign of disturbance brought on by being an only child. Instead, check whether your child's babyish behaviour is in line with what you might expect of children of that age. Here again, it is a great help to have contact with other families to establish a benchmark of what is "normal". If your child's friends also scream when asked to share a toy, you are less likely to worry that your child does too.

If you have chosen to have only one child in order to give them a better chance in life, keep your expectations in check. Only children are not significantly higher achievers than those with one sibling, so though you may have given your child a boost, you should not expect miracles. Be guided by what other people, like teachers, think your child can realistically achieve.

Don't force your child into a mould. Parents naturally have hopes for their children, that they will become a brain surgeon, get to Grade 8 in piano or be a nippy centre forward. When they have several children, if one fails, the others may succeed. An only child means only one chance. It is doubly important therefore to guard against pushing your child in a direction they do not want to go. Give them the opportunity to try out the things you want for them, but don't push it if they are not interested. Better to follow their own interests and career choices and help them succeed in them. That applies even more if you have a girl when you wanted a boy or vice versa. Try not to sex-stereotype them, but, equally, don't be upset if your daughter, however much plied with Meccano and train sets, resolutely sticks to dolls and frilly dresses.

And finally, as one very happy adult only child said:

> Parents of an only child have a special responsibility to recognise that the child is a child, and not just a sort of miniature adult, because I think it is very easy for parents to expect the child to be at their level over everything, and the child probably naturally wants to try and be as grown up as it can; but that defeats the purpose of childhood in a way. I think, ultimately, you don't mature as fully as you would if given the chance to be a child and go through all the phases that a child goes through.

Helping Your Child to Enjoy their own Company

However many friends they have and however much you do things with them, only children have to spend some time on their own. Far from being a disadvantage, that is a good thing. Many children, only or not, relish periods of solitude, and the ability to enjoy your own company is a great asset in life. Reading, working at a hobby, ruminating on the world, or simply letting their imagination have free rein are all good for children.

There is no doubt that some only children take to their own company much more easily than others. (I speak with feeling, having had one of each.) If you have a child who from early on has been happy for some of the time to lie quietly looking at the trees, or to push shapes into slots, you have it made. Just go on providing interesting things for them to do as they get older. But if your child is naturally very sociable, you have more of a problem, as this mother of a seven-year-old explains.

> Rachel didn't want to be on her own as a baby – always wanted to be with her cheek next to yours and needed a lot of physical contact and company. So early on it was quite difficult. She drove me mad – I used to go to about four mother and toddlers groups a week. It was very wearing but I did that for a while because she loved it and she seemed to need the company. Until this year she could only play for five minutes on her own upstairs and then she'd come down, she would need you to see what she was doing or play with her. [*How did you find that?*] Well, it's very demanding really, isn't it? It has just happened now that if she's got something really interesting, she might

go off for half an hour. I'm not quite sure about this, but I get the impression that sometimes she likes being on her own now.

Children like Rachel seem to have to learn to play on their own, and you can help them do so. It won't come quickly. They need input first and you may have to spend a lot of time in the first few years doing things with them to build up a range of interesting things that they can carry on by themselves. You can tell them stories and play "pretend" games with them to develop their own sense of fantasy, so that later on they can play imaginative games with their toys by themselves. You can help them make models, paint alongside them and of course read to them. When they finally do start to play on their own for short periods, you can provide interesting materials, make occasional suggestions and hugely admire the results. Don't take the easy way out and stick them in front of the TV all day. That just reinforces the feeling that they need constant entertainment.

Whichever type of child you have, try to help them find strong lifelong interests in which they can get absorbed. Children and adults are more resilient to circumstances if they can retreat occasionally to a world which they create and control (like boat building, gardening or cooking), as well having interests which bring them into contact with others (like singing and playing sport). Both will stand your only child in good stead in later life. And do encourage them to read – it is one of the few activities that can be done on your own at any place and any time; it is cheap and all absorbing.

Helping your Child to Make and Value Friendships

One of the main differences between only child and sibling children is that only children have to create their own companions. When young, siblings can rely on each other for entertainment – only children have to *make* friends. Since friends, unlike siblings, are not obliged to keep you company, but show a distressing tendency to push off if annoyed, it is a help if your child learns early on how to get on with others. If from the baby stage your only child is used to having other children about, whether at a nursery or a child-minder, or just when you are socialising with other families, they will get the idea that toys have to be shared, turns taken and that they do not always get first choice at the plate of biscuits. But do expect them to make a fuss sometimes – putting other people first is not something that comes easily to small children whether they have siblings or not. Some parents make special efforts to teach only children to share, or to take turns, but it may well just come with time whatever you do. Organised pre-school experience of some sort is very valuable for only children, but it is useful too if they can also have more informal contact with other children in the neighbourhood. If your child has problems joining in, help them, perhaps by fostering a relationship with one child as a stepping stone, inviting the group to your place so they are on your child's home ground, or getting them all involved in some interesting activity.

If only children have that sort of experience before starting school, it is less likely they will have particular problems with other children in the playground. But if they do and your efforts to help them fail, ask you child's teacher for advice. Most teachers nowadays are anxious to nip any kind of teasing and bullying in the bud and have vast experience of dealing with it.

In helping your child acquire the art of making and keeping friends early on, you are setting them up for life. If they develop a growing network of friendships for company and support and can turn in old age to lifelong friends for a sense of shared memories, they are less likely to regret a lack of brothers and sisters. If they have learned to make close, meaningful relationships with other people they will be better equipped to cope with the deaths and disasters that come to us all. Of all the tasks that face the parent of an only child, teaching them to make and value friends is perhaps the most important.

So how can you foster your child's friendships? If you are one of those rare people who are "naturals" with children and attract them like iron filings to a magnet, your child will get off to a flying start. But the rest of us can do a lot too. Once they are at school, let your child choose their own friends and then be positive about them even if they are not the ones you would have chosen. If you are critical of them, either overtly or in more subtle ways, your child will pick that up and will be discouraged. Make your house or flat an attractive place for children. Let your child know that friends are always welcome, and when they arrive make them feel at home. Invite particular friends to spend the night and share special occasions, trips and outings with you. If you can keep open house for other children, not only will your child have plenty of company and practice at relationships, they will acquire from you a habit of opening out to other people, which will stand them in good stead later on.

All this will wreak havoc with the quiet life you may have aimed for in having only one child. You will probably spend a lot of time looking after other people's children, especially in the early days when they all have to be supervised to stop mayhem breaking out. You will almost certainly not get this reciprocated to an equal extent – other families will not necessarily be so open, and sibling children need outside company less than yours. If your child is of above average sociability, you may find the early years quite wearing:

> When Patricia was four, most weekends we'd have local children in – a house full of children. You get to Saturday or Sunday night and you can feel really tired having children bouncing around the house. It really was something, having people around at your house all the time.

But grit your teeth. It is worth it. Gradually, they will calm down, begin to play cooperatively, disappear for hours into the garden. By the time they all reach adolescence, your child will have a widening circle of other teenagers and their families to form an extended friendship network and the pressure will be off.

Of course, friendships do not always go that smoothly. Children fall out as well as in, and the only child who has lost their best friend is a heartrending sight, as this mother of an eleven-year-old explains.

> When he was about seven or eight somebody new came to the class and kind of "took" his best friend. That was hurtful for him and hurtful for us in watching what was happening and seeing how he was affected by that. I think at that point he actually became a bit less confident about making friends. But at the moment there's just a big group of them going round together. He may spend a bit more time with one than with another but they do just tend to go around in a big sort of gang. That's quite nice. We try to encourage him to do that a bit I think, to maintain other friendships so that there's a kind of insurance that if anything went wrong with one particular friendship for some reason. [*Do you think it was worse for him losing that friend, being the only one?*] I think it could be, because if people come home to their brothers and sisters it might give them some sort of security – there would at least be other kids back at home that he would know cared about him in some way. But I don't think he had that and I think it was difficult for him.

We do not in fact know if only children are more distressed than sibling children by loss of a close friend – research shows that all children can become very depressed when that happens. But the comment above seems likely.

That is not to say only children shouldn't have best friends or be exposed to what is a normal childhood upset. But it can be a good idea to encourage your child to diversify their friendships – even if they have a special one, to keep up with others as well. There is safety in numbers. You should also teach your child not to be fickle themselves – that friends, as one of Hawke and Knox's mothers put it, "are not people to use, but people to give to and share with." Of course, that applies to all children, but it is the only child who is in most need of good close friendships throughout life.

Creating Wider Networks

For many only children, the start of school is the time when they realise they are "different" in not having an older or younger brother or sister and, perhaps because of that, it is also a time when the extended family can become very important to them. They want to know about their roots on both sides and to meet and keep in touch with relatives their own age, such as cousins. You can help them by fostering links with your extended family, arranging family gatherings and exchange visits with cousins. Close relationships of this kind help the child to feel they are part of a wider group, and open up contacts with other adults like aunts and uncles, as well as with their children. In later life, cousins can be vitally important to an only child, enabling them to share memories and a sense of family tradition in the way that siblings do. When an only child's parents die, the fact that cousins have known and loved them too can be a great comfort and support. And, as we saw in Chapter 7, cousins can keep each other company in later life.

But you can also create this kind of network for your child by fostering close links with other families – where the whole family become friends, not just the children. If you are lucky enough to be able to keep up friendships of this kind throughout childhood, the other parents become surrogate mums and dads, and your child acquires a whole set of surrogate siblings who can, every bit as much as cousins, provide shared memories, company and support.

Creating close links with other families, whether relatives or not, has other advantages for an only child. If the other family has more than one child, it lets your child experience at first hand what it is like having a sibling. That can be a salutary reminder that the reality does not always match up to the fantasy, but it can also let your child see happy sibling relationships for themselves, help look after babies, watch toddlers growing up and learn how sibling disputes get resolved. All of that helps to keep your child's own family-size options open. It will help them to decide realistically later on whether they want more than one child themselves, and it will give them at least an idea of how a larger family works. It also lets the children from the larger family see what the one-child family is like. The exchange can benefit both sides, as this mother of an adult only child explains.

> We lived just down the road from a family of five. Kathy used to go up there a lot, and she'd just be taken in like one of the family – get her plate of chips along with the rest. She was usually specially pally with one or other of the family, and whoever it was at the time would come down to our place, and paint, or make models, or help in the garden, or whatever we were doing. A bit of peace and quiet.

But as well as the specific advantages these wider networks create, they can also be important for the only child's feelings about the world. When I asked the father of a fifteen-year-old if there were any points he would like to see in my book, he said:

> I think what I would stress is simply the sense of confidence. Giving the child the sense that it's a home they can obviously relate to, but that it's a home that is open to the outside world. That they're not just within a very limited world; that there is a larger world there as well. I think that's very, very important. If you bring them up in that kind of environment, the child gets a sense of confidence. That although she's a single child and it's a small family, she doesn't have to feel that that's the only kind of relationship she can relate to. That there is a broader side to things.

Picking the Right Location and Staying Put

A happy only childhood is likely to involve children in a lot of coming and going between each other's houses. You will make it much easier for yourself and your child if you live among other families, in an area relatively free from traffic where children can go about independently. A housing estate, a village or a quiet town street are all ideal. That pretty cottage, perched on a hill, miles from nowhere, is not. It may sound fun, but it can be very isolating for a child. They cannot get to their friends without you taking them; more difficult still, friends cannot get to to your home unless their parents bring them (or you fetch them). If you pick a location like that, be prepared for a lot of chauffeuring into late adolescence.

For similar reasons, think hard before deciding not to send your child to the local school. The social disadvantages may outweigh any educational benefits. Your child may find it more difficult to mix in with local children, and school friends may be too far to visit easily.

Nor is it ideal for an only child to be always moving. You may have no option but to go where the work is, but don't move just for the sake of it. Every time you do, you disrupt your child's friendships, and make it harder for them to keep up the kind of close long-term relationships they need. Similar considerations apply to moving schools.

Having said that, it is obviously not just a question of geography. Some occupations that involve frequent moves develop, in compensation, strongly supportive social systems, which they carry with them wherever they go, and which can be very good for only children.

> My father was in the army and we moved around a lot, so I think we belonged to quite a close community anyway. We were all part of the regiment. There was a lot of to-ing and fro-ing. Joint taking care of kids, and family events, Sunday lunchtime in the mess, that kind of thing. So perhaps that made up for not having brothers and sisters of your own. I think it was quite a supportive community and quite a close community, so maybe that gave you quite a good start. I was certainly not aware of ever feeling lonely as a child or anything like that.

Planning for your Child on Holidays, Trips and Special Occasions

As we saw in Chapter 4, holidays and special occasions like Christmas present something of a challenge to one-child families. Since they are thought of as a time for family, even children with many close friends will probably spend them with their parents. If parents and child share interests, the parents are great fun to be with and go out of their way to make it a child-centred occasion, that can work well. However, most children find a holiday more enjoyable if they can spend at least some of the time with others of a similar age. As one of Hawke and Knox's mothers said, "Children see things differently than adults and they have more fun when they have experiences together. Besides, they entertain each other and give parents a chance to enjoy things in their own way."

Because of this, some one-child parents always take another child along when they go on holidays or trips. My own parents did that – sometimes it would be a favourite cousin, other times my current best friend. It worked very well, because my parents had a gift for children, and the other child always had a good time. It is obviously important not to use the child as an unpaid companion to yours; you have to concentrate on seeing they enjoy themselves too. For that reason, other parents feel it is better if their child goes alone with them and makes holiday friends.

> People keep saying, "Do you not take somebody with you for her?" and I say "No". I couldn't stand it at this stage because I think to look after another child for a fortnight who would maybe get homesick or maybe not like what we are doing, it would be difficult. It would really make it more fraught. I feel it wouldn't be a holiday because you would have to be concerned about this other child's needs; it's different when they're older, if they didn't want to do something you wanted, they could do something else.

Instead, they choose a holiday location where they will be sure of plenty of other children – in this case, camping holidays in France.

> That was good because when you are in tents and you're living with each other they always find someone to play with, even while you're getting the dinner ready, or you can send them to wash up the dishes at the communal wash up and they meet another child or other people. [*And did Katy manage to strike up friendships?*] Yes, quite easily. You always take bats and balls, and kind of after dinner everyone appeared you know, hitting the balls, everyone joined in. There wasn't a language problem. I found children played happily, similar games. But then she's very good at making friends. There's no problem about having to take her to people and try and make it work.

If your child is very sociable, that is obviously a good solution. But it may not be so easy if they are shy or if you choose a different type of holiday setting. You then risk them not being able to find a friend for the whole holiday.

A compromise solution is to team up with another family, either friends or relatives, and go together. The children have each other to play with, but they also have their own parents for comfort. The adults can take turns babysitting in the evening, or taking the children off for a trip, leaving the other pair free to do their own thing. Again, this can work fine, especially if the other family is part of your "wider network" and you know them well.

Which option is best for you will obviously depend on your child's personality and age, on how much you enjoy the company of other people's children, and of course on your finances. But whatever you do, remember that it is your child's holiday too and see that they enjoy themselves.

The same considerations apply to shorter trips. Only children can often get more fun out of a trip to the zoo, the theatre or the beach if a friend comes along, and if you are lucky the friend's family will reciprocate. But don't go mad and feel you have to take another child everywhere you go. If your ten-year-old has a passion for un-accompanied Bach cello sonatas, they will probably enjoy the concert more on their own with you than with a friend fidgeting beside them.

Is Christmas a problem for only children? It clearly is for some:

> Because even though you got all these presents it was great, they did play with you, but if you got a game and there's two people and one's making the dinner and one's doing something else, who have you got to play with?

Nor is a group of elderly relatives necessarily much fun for a child, though I would argue that that depends on the elderly relatives. Getting together with another family and taking turns to host a Christmas Day or Christmas holiday is one possibility that works well. Another is a big extended family get-together. If you or your child want a large number of children around the turkey, they don't all have to be home reared.

Helping Your Child Feel Good about their Status

There are only children around who have never wanted a sibling, but they must be in the minority. Most parents sooner or later face the double question: "Why haven't I got a brother or sister?" and "Can we have one?"

These questions tend not to arise in the first few years. It takes a child some time to realise that being the only one is different, and in any case many of their friends have no siblings either to start with. It's likely to come up as an issue around the time they start school, and that's lucky, because by that time most children are able to understand and accept an explanation if it is put reasonably. Experienced parents suggest that the best approach is to be as honest as is consistent with being positive. If the real reason is something like a very bad experience at birth or severe postnatal depression, you do not have to go into the gory details, but you could take the line that this mother did:

> He said something about why do some people have brothers and sisters and I told him that I was very ill after I had him and I didn't want to be ill again if I had another baby and he just seemed to accept that.

Make sure the child knows it is just something that happens sometimes and that it wasn't anything they were responsible for.

If you had one child through choice, there will probably be a number of reasons for it, and you can choose which one to use. You can explain that you enjoy having one child very much and do not feel you would be so good at looking after two or three. If finance or housing have entered into your decision, you could mention that, as you could things like population concerns. But the fact that your child wailed night and day and that you never want to go through it again is best left until they are old enough to laugh about it with you. It is important that your child doesn't think that you are not having another child because you are unhappy with them.

Some children seem to ask once and forget about it. Others will argue the point. If they do, you could explain that how many children to have is just one of the decisions that parents have to make themselves, because it is they who have to look after them.

What if your child goes on desperately hankering for a baby brother or sister? First of all, remind yourself that they are not being deprived of something fundamental that will ruin their lives, so you don't need to feel guilty. Don't buy them things "to make up for" not having a sibling – they don't need it and it will only confirm them in the belief that they are indeed missing out. Do check that you are giving them plenty of time, attention and fun and that they have good contacts with extended family and friends. Try to arrange for them to spend some time helping look after other people's babies instead. Best of all, have a younger child over to stay – so that they can see the reality rather than the dream. See if you can find some other only children for them to meet so that they can see they are not alone in lacking siblings. Point out that brothers and sisters quarrel as well as play.

Then relax. Children hanker after many things that "everyone else has" – a pony, a pair of trainers with the right labels, a white curly lamb coat. In a situation where, realistically, most other people do have siblings it is natural for them to feel they are missing out. But though they may want a brother or sister, they do not need one. And if they have a good life as an only child, the hankering will probably pass.

> Natalie has an imaginary little sister who she produces on occasions. She walks home from school a part of the way on her own now. I meet her, and when I met her one day I said "What have you been doing?" She said "Oh I've been talking to my imaginary little sister, she's in Primary Two, and we were talking about how it's a nasty wet day today and we were looking forward to getting home." And I was filled with guilt about this and so I said "I'm sorry, Natalie, because I know in some ways you would have liked to have had a little sister," because she would. And she said "No! Actually in some ways I think I'd prefer to have an imaginary one because when I'm fed up with her I can tell her to go away!"

Not Worrying about the Myths

I have talked a lot about popular attitudes and the negative stereotype of the only child. Such attitudes do exist but they are of course not universal, and they seem to pass many only children and their parents by. I only became conscious of them myself eight years ago, by which time I had been an only child for forty five years, had reared one only child and embarked on another. However, since I have been doing research on the subject I have more than made up for it. Casual mention at parties has produced about 50 per cent real interest, 10 per cent joyful recognition from other only children or one-child parents, 10 per cent uncomfortable silence and 20 per cent hot air as people let loose the prejudices of a lifetime.

So if you are one of the unlucky ones who have been criticised for your choice of an only child, or who are aware of snide comments, I sympathise. Such remarks are very upsetting. What should you do about it?

Many parents of only children choose just to ignore criticism and that's certainly the easiest option. Think of it as bad manners, or as the remark of some poor benighted soul who knows no better. Smile in a superior way which implies you do. But if you want to answer a direct comment with one of your own, I hope this book will give you appropriate ammunition. "It's very interesting you should mention that", you can say, leaning earnestly forward, "because in fact research shows ..." I have found that quite an effective gambit, and have even made a few converts. On the other hand, it will not silence everyone. "You surely don't imagine that I am going to be convinced by *proof*?" said a scornful cartoon wife to her husband, who was reaching for the encyclopedia. When people are that bound up in myths, nothing will shift them and there is not a lot you can do about it. Write it off.

Above all, don't worry. I hope this book will have convinced you that the vast majority of the myths are without foundation. Only children are not in general maladjusted, lonely or spoiled and you are not selfish in having one. People, for reasons I have suggested, have simply got it wrong.

Don't Assume it's Easy!

If the above suggestions seem a tall order, that is realistic. The common belief that being an only child is an easier option is one that many one-child parents would dispute. True, you avoid the hassle of juggling the needs and wants of two or more children of differing years and temperaments. The dirty nappies are fewer and so are the sleepless nights. But being the parent of an only child has its own tasks and obligations, as this one-child father who came from a large family points out.

> I would say it's great only having one child from one point of view, it's great because as a parent you don't have to try and split loyalties and emotions and what not. The focus is on the one, so it's great in that respect. On the other hand, it could be not so great because of the commitment you have really got to show. When you get back from work and you're tired and they say "You said we could have a game of cards," and there's no other children for you to say "Play with your brother or your sister." I feel your obligations are also part of it. When you've only one child, they've got to play. If there's no child for them to play with you've just got to play with them.

Being the parent of an only child means playing with them even when you don't feel like it. It means sharing your leisure time with them. It means having other people's children about the house and on holiday with you. For those reasons, it is not a good option for people who don't like children. If you genuinely cannot be bothered with them, the right number of children to have is not one. It is none.

But what if you had a child under the impression you liked them and then discovered that babies were not for you? Don't despair. Few parents are equally adept at every age. Although at the time it seems to go on for ever, the baby stage is in fact brief and untypical of the rest of childhood, and the fact that you found it difficult does not mean you will be a failure later on. Ironically, the qualities of detachment and interest in the outside world that made it hard for you to mother a baby, can make you a superb parent for a teenager. Better that way round than to have six children because you love babies and then discover you can't stand adolescents.

Of course, what this chapter presents is an ideal list of ingredients for an only childhood. For thousands of years children have been growing up satisfactorily in circumstances that are only "good enough", and the same is true of only children. The fact that they turn out so very much like other small-family children suggests that producing a well-adjusted only child is no more complicated and difficult than bringing up two. Given a reasonable relationship with at least one parent, not overindulged, and encouraged to become independent, any child is likely to turn out well.

However, producing an only child *who is happy to be an only child* may take a bit more thought. There are many adult only children around who, while apparently leading perfectly satisfactory lives, nonetheless feel they have missed out from not having siblings. There are others who have no regrets. We do not know what distinguishes unregretful from regretful only children, but from my encounters over the years I have a hunch it may be to do with the kinds of things we have been looking at in this chapter.

Though their experiences vary enormously, those who feel good about being an only child seem to have had at least some of the following: close, confiding relationships with positive parents who had realistic expectations, were fun to be with, who spent a lot of time with their child but who encouraged independence; plenty of friends their own age and freedom to meet them; an outgoing family style that included other parents and children; strong interests; and circumstances which enabled them to retain relationships with family, friends and neighbours into later life.

In contrast, only children who regret their status often seem to have had childhoods lacking in many of these qualities, being indeed, as they complain: lonely or overprotected, with parents who were either smothering, dominating, cool, or simply rather unimaginative. That sort of childhood is not, of course, calculated to cheer anyone, only or not. However, it seems possible that good parenting may be especially important to only children, since there is no one else to dilute a bad experience.

For that reason, I sometimes worry about only children at the turn of this century. Not that they will turn out any less well adjusted or contented as adults, but that they may look back on their childhoods with little pleasure. In some ways, things have improved for only children over the past few decades. Organised pre-school experience will have reduced the likelihood of a child being isolated or unable to get on with other children and reduced the shock of starting school. Clubs, after school activities and school camps also provide more opportunities for socialising. Increased car ownership means that children can (if chauffeured) keep in touch with friends who are at a distance.

But in other ways, life may be more difficult. Families move around more from house to house or town to town, disrupting their children's friendships. Traffic hazards and fears of "stranger danger" now keep many children off the street and confined to their homes in front of the TV or the computer; they no longer have the freedom to wander in and out of each other's houses, casually join in informal street play, or roam the countryside as they used to. Entertainment has become progressively home-based, with fewer opportunities for going out and meeting other families. With an increase in two-career couples, parents are spending only half as much time with their children as they did thirty years ago: "The nuclear family has been replaced by the nuclear child, alone in its centrally heated bedroom" (*Independent on Sunday*, 17 October 1993).

In that context, it is possible that only children may indeed be deprived of the ingredients for a happy childhood. It is a concern if today's parents choose to have an only child under the impression that one will have less impact, and if they then proceed to lead their adult lives without reference to the child's needs. Their child will probably still turn out fine, but may not thank them for it later on.

Parents have a right to choose the family size that suits them best, but they have a corresponding responsibility to make sure that the experience is a happy one for their child. A good childhood can warm you for the rest of your life, and all children deserve one. Every only child should be able to say:

> I had an absolutely super childhood and I had a wonderful youth. And, I can say that quite honestly. I've had a lovely life since, but you know, looking back I think – gosh I was lucky.

Summing-up

In most respects, bringing up an only child is just like bringing up a child from any other family size, and the fact that only children turn out every bit as well as those with siblings suggests that there is nothing particularly difficult about it. However, raising a child who feels good about being the only one may present more of a challenge. Though there is no systematic research evidence for it, many one-child parents and adult only children feel that there are some strategies that will help an only child turn out well and look back with pleasure on their childhood. (Of course, many of them would benefit children with siblings, too.)

- Be positive about having an only child.
- Create a good relationship with your child – one that is warm, involved and fairly egalitarian.
- Encourage your child to become independent and avoid becoming dependent on them.
- Avoid overindulgence – limit material possessions and fattening foods and deal firmly with bad behaviour.
- Keep expectations realistic – don't pressure your child into prematurely adult behaviour, or into fulfilling your dreams for them. Remember to treat your child as a child.
- Help your child to enjoy their own company and to build up interests for later life.
- Help them to acquire the art of getting on with people, making friends and being a good friend themselves.
- Foster contacts with your extended family and create links with other families.
- Pick a child-friendly environment and, if possible, stay there.
- Find childhood company for your child on holidays, trips and special occasions.
- Help your child to accept and feel good about being an only child.

- Don't believe in the myths yourself.
- Don't assume that having an only child will make less impact on your adult life – in some ways, it can be harder work. If you are older parents or have very busy careers, make sure you allow enough time, space and energy to give your only child a really good experience.

Is there an Ideal Family Size?

We have come a long way from our original question: "Is it selfish to have an only child?" All the evidence suggests that it is not. Contrary to popular and "expert" beliefs, growing up without brothers and sisters appears to do you no harm at all. Only children seem to turn out as well-adjusted and as able to get on with other people as anyone else. They are as happy and satisfied with life as sibling children, and they are no more socially isolated. They certainly get more in the way of parental time and attention, but that doesn't seem to harm their personal and social development, and may even benefit their academic motivation and self-esteem. They appear to have no particular problems in achieving independence, and to be no less satisfactory as marriage partners and parents. The worst you could say, on the basis of present evidence, is that in childhood some of them have a tendency to put on weight, and that in adulthood male only children may find it more stressful coping with elderly parents.

Nor is there much evidence that only children are more at risk in particular circumstances. In adoptive families only children seem to do as well as those with siblings, and in one-parent families they may even do better. It is quite possible that it is worse being an only child in a disturbed and abusing family, but there is no real evidence of that.

Are there no advantages at all in having brothers and sisters? There does seem to be one – it gives you the chance to experience one of life's major relationships. Many people who have siblings feel there is something very special about the bond beween them; a unique link, which at best runs enjoyably throughout life from beginning to end. Only children miss out on that. But then sibling children miss out on the chance of an uninterrupted, undivided loving relationship with their parents. You can't open one door without closing the other.

Although our society decrees that two children (and one of each sex) is the ideal family size, there is in fact no such thing. Have one, and your child may have to care for you single handed in old age. Have two, and they may run into problems of competitiveness and jealousy.

Have three or more, and you are diminishing the amount of time and energy you have for each child. There is no perfect family size, only horses for courses.

Diversity of family size is good, not only because it makes life more interesting, but because it allows parents to pick the size of family that suits them best. The choice between one and two makes little or no difference to the child, but it may make a considerable difference to the parents. They may justifiably feel that it is easier to provide their child with a package of companionship and support in the shape of a sibling, rather than to help them establish other relationships to take on those functions. They may prefer their child to play predominantly with a brother or sister, rather than with other children outside the family. They may feel it will be more fun for them as parents if there are more children around, or they may want the joy of seeing two people who are a part of them relating lovingly to each other. They may want to have more than one child as insurance against losing either of them. They may even want to ensure that at least one of their children will be willing to support them in old age.

All these are perfectly valid reasons for having two or more children, and there is nothing in this book to challenge them, apart from pointing out that it doesn't always work out like that. But they are no more "unselfish" than the reasons parents give for wanting only one. What research does is to debunk the myth that having more than one child is a morally superior option; that it is better for the child.

This book has presented an upbeat picture of only children. That is justified. The reality is that they do tend to turn out well and to be happy and satisfied with life. That doesn't mean, of course, that all only children are happy and well-adjusted; there clearly are some who are not. What research shows is that only children who fit the stereotype are a tiny minority. They are not "typical only children". There is no such thing as a typical only child. Only children are like everyone else in that they are all different. Some are sociable, some are shy. Some are easy going, some are exacting. Some are high achievers, others struggle along. It's not just being an only child that makes you what you are. It's the genetic blueprint you are born with, the society you live in, the way your parents bring you up, the friends you make, the jobs you get, the partner you marry, the children you have, and all the myriad chance experiences you encounter along the way. And those influences are there for all children, whatever their family size.

Recommended Reading

Falbo, T. (ed.), *The Single Child Family,* New York, Guilford Press, 1984.
Contains descriptions of several of the major research studies cited in this book, and starts with a first-rate review by Toni Falbo of research up to 1980. Aimed at social scientists and professionals rather than parents, but not too technical. Denise Polit's chapter on one-parent/one-child families is particularly good.

Hawke, S. and Knox, D., *One Child by Choice,* Prentice Hall, 1977.
A well-balanced, highly readable book aimed at parents, but unfortunately out of print. Contains an extensive, but untechnical, review of the research up to the mid-1970s, and continues with a very fair discussion of the pros and cons of having an only child, based on the experiences of only children and one-child parents of all ages. It concludes with a section of advice about only children at different stages of development, again based on the experiences of one-child parents.

Foltz Jones, C., *Only Child: Clues for Coping,* Westminster Press, 1984.
A book addressed to only children of about 8 upwards. Despite its uninspiring title it is very entertaining and readable. It focuses on reassuring only children about their status, helping them to deal with the myths, and giving them tips for making the most of their situation.

Dunn, J. and Plomin, R., *Separate Lives: Why Siblings are so Different,* New York, Basic Books, 1990.
Anything by Judy Dunn is worth reading, but this is interesting for the very balanced picture it gives of the reality behind the sibling myth.

Notes

Every research study described in this book is listed in the References section under its author and date. However, to make the book more readable for a general audience, I have not always cited authors and dates of research studies in the text. Any that are not clearly identified are given here, under the appropriate chapter heading. When you have located the author's name and date, go to the References section to get fuller details of where the study was published.

Introduction

Page reference

1. Opening quote: Bert Lance, *Nation's Business* 27 May, 1977
1. "To me one is not a family ...", Busfield and Paddon, 1977, p. 146.
2-3. Biographics: Jean Rook, *The Cowardly Lioness*; Gordon Kaye and Hilary Bonner, *Rene and Me*; Jonathon Margolis, *Cleese Encounters*; Roy Plomley, *Days seemed Longer*; Rita Hunter, *Wait till the Sun Shines, Nellie*; Robert Rhodes James, *Bob Boothby*.
4. Royal Commission on the Family, 1949.
4. Declining popularity of one-child family: Werner and Chalk, 1986.
4. Stereotype a major reason for having at least two children: Busfield and Paddon, 1977; Cartwright, 1976; Askham, 1975.
4. EEC surveys: description in *Family Policy Bulletin*, August 1991.
5. Expected family size: General Household Survey, 1994.
6. Study of media references: Laybourn, 1990a.

7. Books based on the experiences of adult only children: Hawke and Knox, 1977, Sifford, 1989.

9. National Child Development Study (NCDS): carried out by the National Children's Bureau. The dataset is held by the ESRC Data Archive at the University of Essex. Those who carried out the original analysis and collection of the data bear no responsibility for the secondary analysis of it carried out for this book, nor for the opinions expressed in it.

9-10. NCDS research on influence of family size, also information on losses from original sample: Fogelman, 1983a; Kiernan, 1992.

Chapter 1

14. Opening quote: from Combaluzier, 1954.

14. Popular attitudes to one-child parents: Polit, 1978.

14. One-child parents in the USA: Cutts and Moseley, 1954; Falbo, 1978; Wilson and Knox, 1981; Gee, 1992; Polit, 1984.

15. Scottish one-child parents: Laybourn, 1990a.

15. NCDS one-child families: Ferri, 1976, and analysis for this book.

15. Responses to opinion polls on reasons for one child: Pankhurst, 1982.

16. Financial reasons for both one and two children: Katz and Boswell, 1984.

17. Profit and loss accounts: for summary and references, see Callan, 1985.

17-18. Reasons for having an only child in the USA: Hawke and Knox, 1977; Katz and Boswell, 1984. In Australia: Callan, 1985.

21. Research on siblings: e.g. Dunn and Plomin, 1990.

21. Only children tend to opt for smaller families: Groat et al, 1984.

21. Only children and ideal family size: Ware, 1973.

22. More likely to have one (French census): Desplanques, 1993.

24. Parents more likely to stop at one if a boy: Katz and Boswell, 1984; Groat et al, 1984.

25. Easier for only girls to fit parental expectations: Katz and Boswell, 1984.

Chapter 2.

29. Quantitative review of ability and achievement: Polit and Falbo, 1988.

30. Debate about family size and ability/achievement: Blake, 1989 .

31. Experiments challenging tutoring hypothesis: Falbo and Snell, 1982.

31. First child not more intelligent than the second: Ernst and Angst, 1983.

32. Children of lone parents do less well: e.g. Dawson, 1991. Reasons for this, e.g. Ferri, 1976.

34. Canadian women's educational and occupational levels: Gee, 1992.

Chapter 3.

36. Opening quote: attributed to G. Stanley Hall. Quoted in Fenton 1928.

37. 1922 psychoanalyst; Brill, 1922.

37. Specialist in birth order psychology: Toman 1969.

37. Authoritative psychiatric textbook: Million, 1981.

39-40. Early research and psychiatric research: for a comprehensive review, see Ernst and Angst, 1983.

41. Overview by Falbo: 1984a.

41. Quantitative review of personality and behaviour: Polit and Falbo, 1987; Falbo, 1992.

44. Home and School Behaviour tests show up differences and predict psychiatric disturbance: Rutter, 1970; Ghodsian et al, 1980; Fogelman 1983.

45. Only children, friendships and peer popularity: Falbo, 1984a; Falbo and Polit, 1986; Blake, 1989.

45. Sibling and peer-group relationships: Dunn and McGuire, 1992.

46-47. Chinese studies: Poston and Yu, 1984; Jiao, Ji and Jing, 1986; Falbo et al, 1986; Falbo and Poston, 1993; Meredith et al, 1989; Falbo, 1992.

48. Chinese parents with one child are different: Bakken, 1993.

48. Chinese children introduce selves by birth order: Falbo and Poston, 1993.

Chapter 4.

49. Opening quote: F. B. and E.G. Gilbreth, *Cheaper by the Dozen,* Heinemann Ltd, 1949.

50. Australian women on loneliness: Ware, 1973.

55. Polit study of couples with teenage children: Polit et al, 1980.

60. US surveys of adult satisfaction and happiness: Glen and Hoppe, 1984.

60. Sibling research: Dunn and Kendrick 1982, Dunn and Plomin, 1990.

Chapter 5.

62. Opening quote: attributed to E. W. Bohannon. Quoted in Fenton 1928.

65. Sociology student study of parental "regulation": Kloepper et al, 1981.

66. Psychology undergraduate study: Watson and Biderman, 1989.

66. Study of 4th–8th grade children: Stiller, 1990.

67. First time parents have higher expectations: Falbo and Polit, 1986.

69. Canadian study of psychiatric-clinic children: Howe and Madgett, 1975.

70. Falbo and Polit review of parent-child relationships: 1986.

72. Obesity in only children: Jacoby et al 1975, Vuille and Mellbin, 1979.

73. Teenage obesity leads to problems: Gortmaker et al, 1993.

73. Hypertension study: Trevisan et al, 1991.

Chapter 6

74. Opening quote: Interview source.

75. Research on marriage and birth order: Ernst and Angst, 1983.

77. Polit study of married couples: Polit et al 1980.

78. British studies of carers: Lewis and Meredith 1988 (quote), Quereshi and Walker, 1989; Levin et al, 1989.

80. US study of carers: Coward and Dwyer, 1990.

81. Research on ageing: Wenger, 1984 (closer to siblings); Jerrome, 1981 (closer to friends); Cicirelli, 1982 (sources of support); Matthews, 1986 (friendships in old age).

82-83. One-parent/one-child families: Weiss, 1979; Polit, 1984.

83. Lone-parent families in Scotland: Laybourn, 1990a.

84. Adoption: Siegal, 1989; Raynor, 1980.

Chapter 8.

104. The ideas in this chapter come from a variety of sources, among them: Peck, 1977; Falbo, 1992; Falbo et al, 1986; Almodovar, 1973; Blake, 1989.

112. Magazine article with photograph: Laybourn, 1990b.

113. Infant reading scheme: *Link-up Build-up Book 9b* (p. 9), Holmes McDougall.

114. Cognitive dissonance as an explanation: suggested by Dr Beth Alder, Napier University, Edinburgh.

References

Adler, A. 1928. "Characteristics of the first, second and third child" *Children,* 3, pp. 14–52

Almodovar, J.–P. 1973. "Existe-t-il un syndrome de l'enfant unique?" *Enfance,* pp. 235–249

Askham, J. 1975. *Fertility and Deprivation,* Cambridge: Cambridge University Press

Bakken, B. 1993 "Prejudice and danger: the only child in China", *Childhood,* 1, pp. 46–61

Blake, J. 1981. "Family size and the quality of children", *Demography,* 18 18(4), pp. 421–442

Blake, J. 1989, *Family Size and Achievement,* Berkely: University of California Press

Blood, R. O. 1972. *The Family,* New York: Free Press

Bohannon, E. W. 1898. "The only child in a family", *Journal of Genetic Psychology,* 5, pp. 155–164

Brill, A. A. 1922, *Psychoanalysis – its theories and practical applications,* Philadelphia: Saunders

Busfield, J. and Paddon, M. 1977. *Thinking about Children,* Cambridge: Cambridge University Press

Callan, V. 1985. "Comparisons of mothers of one child by choice with mothers wanting a second birth", *Journal of Marriage and the Family,* 47 (1), pp. 155–64

Cartwright, A. 1976. *How Many Children?,* London: Routledge Kegan Paul

Cicirelli, V. G. 1982. "Sibling influence throughout the lifespan", *Sibling Relationships: Their Nature and Significance Across the Lifespan* (ed.) Lamb, M. E. and Sutton Smith, B., N. J. : Lawrence Erlbaum Associates

Claudy, J. G. 1984. "The only child as young adult" in Falbo 1984b

Combaluzier, C. 1954. *L'Enfant Seul* (Cahiers due centre Laennée), Paris: Letheilleux (Quoted in Almodovar 1973)

Cooper, J. and Shaw, C. 1993. . "Fertility assumptions for the 1991–based national population projections", *Population Trends,* 71

Coward, R. T. and Dwyer, J. W. 1990. "The association of gender, sibling network composition and patterns of parent care by adult children", *Research on Ageing,* Vol 12(2), pp. 158–181

Cutts, N. and Moseley, N. 1954. *The Only Child,* New York: G. P. Putnam's Sons

Dawson, D. A. 1991. "Family structure and children's mental health and well-being", *Journal of Marriage and the Family,* 53 pp. 573–584

Desplanques, G. 1993. "Plus diplomes et de plus en plus nombreux", *L'Evénement du Jeudi,* 6–12 Mai, p. 71

Dunn, J. and Kendrick, C. 1982. *Siblings, Love, Envy and Understanding,* Cambridge, Mass: Harvard University Press

Dunn, J. and McGuire, S. 1992. "Sibling and peer relationships in childhood", *Journal of Child Psychology and Psychiatry,* 31(1), pp. 67–105

Dunn, J. and Plomin, R. 1990. *Separate Lives*, New York: Basic Books

Ernst, L. and Angst, J. 1983. *Birth Order: Its Influence on Personality*, Springer Verlag

Falbo, T. 1978. "Reasons for having an only child", *Journal of Population*, 1(2) pp. 181–184

Falbo, T. 1984a. "Only children: a review" in Falbo 1984b

Falbo, T. (ed.) 1984b. *The Single-child Family*, New York: The Guilford Press

Falbo, T. 1992. "Social norms and the one-child family: clinical and policy implications", in *Children's Sibling Relationships: Developmental and Clinical Issues*, Boer, F. and Dunn, J. Hillsdale, N. J. : Lawrence Erlbaum Associates Inc.

Falbo, T. and Cooper, C. R. 1980. "Young children's time and intellectual ability", *Journal of Genetic Psychology*, 173, pp. 299–300

Falbo, T., Jiao, S., Ji, G. and Jing, Q. 1986, *Only Children in China*, Texas Population Research Center Papers

Falbo, T. and Polit, D. F. 1986. "Quantitative review of the only child literature: research evidence and theory development", *Psychological Bulletin*, 100(2), pp. 176–189

Falbo, T. and Poston, D. L. 1993. "The academic, personality and physical outcomes of only children in China", *Child Development*, 64(1), pp. 18–35

Falbo, T. and Snell, W. E. 1982. "Experimental tests of the sibling tutoring factor", in Falbo 1984b

Fenton, N. 1928. "The Only Child", *Journal of Genetic Psychology*, 35, pp. 546–556

Ferri, E. 1976. *Growing up in a One-parent Family: a Long-term Study of Child Development*, Windsor, Bucks: NFER Publishing Co Ltd

Fogelman, K. 1983a. "Social class and family size", in Fogelman 1983b

Fogelman, K. 1983b. *Growing up in Great Britain: papers from the National Child Development Study*, (ed.) Fogelman, K., London: MacMillan

Gee, E. M. 1992. "Only children as adult women: life course events and timing", *Social Indicators Research* 26(2), pp. 183–197

Ghodsian, M., Fogelman, K., Lambert, L., and Tibbenham, A. 1980. "Changes in the behaviour ratings of a national sample of children", *British Journal of Social and Clinical Psychology*, 19

Glenn, N. D. and Hoppe, S. K. 1984. "Only children as adults: psychological well-being", *Journal of Family Issues*, 5(3), pp. 363–382

Gortmaker, S. L., Must, A., Perrin, J. M., Sobol, A . M. and Dietz, W. H. 1993. "Social and economic consequences of overweight in adolescence and young adulthood", *New England Journal of Medicine*, 329(14)

Groat, H. T., Wicks, J. W., Neal, A. G. 1984. "Without siblings: the consequences in adult life of having been an only child", in Falbo 1984b

Hawke, S. and Knox, D. 1977. *One Child by Choice*, New Jersey: Prentice Hall

Hogan, R. A., Kirchner, J. H., Hogan, K. A., Fox, A. N. 1980. "The only child factor in homosexual development", *Psychology*, 17(1), pp.19–33

Howe, M. G. and Madgett, M. E. 1975. "Mental health problems associated with the only child", *Canadian Psychiatric Association Journal*, 20(3), pp. 189 194

Jacoby, A., Altman, D. G., Cook, J. and Holland, W. W. 1975, "Influence of some social and environmental factors on the nutrient intake and nutritional status of school children", *British Journal of Preventative Social Medicine*, 29, pp. 116–120

Jerrome, D. 1981. "The significance of friendship for women in later life", *Aging and Society*, 1(2), pp. 175–197

Jiao, S., Ji, G. and Jing, Q. 1986. "Comparative study of behavioural qualities of only children and sibling children", *Child Development*, 57(2), pp. 357–361

Kappelman, M. 1975. *Raising the Only Child*, New York: Dutton and Co

Katz, P. and Boswell, S. 1984. "Sex role development and the one-child family", in Falbo 1984b

Kiernan, K. E. 1992. "The impact of family disruption in childhood on transitions made in young adult life", *Population Studies*, 46, pp.213–234

Kloepper, H. W., Leonard, W. M. and Huang, L. J. 1981."A comparison of the only child's and the siblings' perceptions of parental norms and sanctions", *Adolescence*, XVI (63), pp. 641–655

Laybourn, A. 1990a. "Only children in Britain: popular stereotype and research evidence", *Children and Society*, 4(4), pp. 386–400

Laybourn, A. 1990b. "Only children", *Scottish Child*, June/July

Levin, E., Sinclair, I., and Gorbeck, P. 1989. *Families, Services and Confusion in Old Age*, Avebury

Lewis, J. and Meredith, B. 1988. *Daughters Who Care*, London: Routlege

Lewis, M. and Feiring, C. 1982. "Some American families at dinner", in L. M. Laosa and I. E. Sigel (eds) *Families as Learning Environments for Children*, pp. 115–145, New York: Plenum Press

Matthews, S. H. 1986. *Friendships Through the Life Course: Oral Biographies in Old Age*, Sage

Mellor, S. 1990. "How do only children differ from other children?", *Journal of Genetic Psychology*, 151(2), pp. 221–230

Meredith, W. H., Abbot, D. A. and Lu Ting Zu. 1989. "A comparative study of only children and sibling children in the People's Republic of China", *School Psychology International*, 10(4), pp.251–256

Million, T. 1981. *Disorders of Personality*, John Wiley and Sons

Pankhurst, J. G. 1982. "Childless and one-child families in the Soviet Union", *Journal of Family Issues*, 3(4), pp. 493–515

Peck, E. 1977. *The Joy of the Only Child*, New York: Delacorte Press

Pitkeathly, J. and Emerson, D. 1994. *Only Child: How to Survive Being One*, London: Souvenir Press

Polit, D. F. 1978. "Stereotypes relating to family size", *Journal of Marriage and the Family*, 40, pp. 105–114

Polit, D. F. 1984. "The only child in single parent families", in Falbo, T. 1984b

Polit, D. F. and Falbo, T. 1987. "Only children and personality development: a quantitative review", *Journal of Marriage and the Family*, 49,pp. 309–325

Polit, D. F. and Falbo, T. 1988. "The intellectual achievement of only children", *Journal Biosocial Science*, 20(3), pp. 275–285

Polit, D. F., Nuttall, R. L. and Nuttall, E. V. 1980. "The only child grows up: a look at some characteristics of adult only children", *Family Relations*, 29, pp. 99–106

Poston, D. and Yu, M. Y. 1984. *Quality of Life, Intellectual Development and Behavioural Characteristics of Single children in China: evidence from a 1980 Survey in Chang Shi Hunnan Province*, Population Research Center University of Texas at Austin

Quereshi, H. and Walker, A. 1989. *The Caring Relationship*, Macmillan

Raynor, L. 1980. *The Adopted Child Comes of Age*, Allen and Unwin

Riley, B 1994. *The Experience of Parenting Only Children*, M. A. Thesis University of East Anglia (in preparation)

Royal Commission on the Decline of the Birth Rate in New South Wales (1904), quoted in Ware, H (1973) op cit

Rutter, M., Tizard, J. and Whitmore, K. 1970. *Education, Health and Behaviour*, Longman

Shanghai Preschool Education Study Group 1980. "Family education of only children", *Chinese Women*, 5, 17

Siegal, S. E. 1989. *Parenting Your Adopted Child – a Complete and Loving Guide*, New York: Prentice Hall Press

Sifford, D. 1989. *The Only Child: Being One, Loving One, Understanding One, Raising One*, New York: G. P. Putnam's Sons

Skynner, R. and Cleese, J. 1983. *Families and How to Survive Them*, London: Methuen

Stiller, L. P. 1990. *An Empirical Analysis of Attributional Thought, Perceived Parent Characteristics and Achievement in Only Children*, PhD Thesis, University of California, LA

Titmuss, R. and Titmuss, K. 1942. *Parents Revolt*, Secker and Warburg

Toman, W. 1969. *Family Constellation: its Effects on Personality and Social Behaviour*, New York: Springer Publishing Co. 2nd edition

Trevisan, M , Krogh, V., Klimovski, L., Bland, S. and Winkelstein, W. 1991. "Absence of siblings: a risk factor for hypertension", *New England Journal of Medicine*, 324(18), p.1285

Veenhoven, R. and Verkuyten, M. 1989. "The well-being of only children", *Adolescence* XXIV(93), pp. 155–166

Vuille, J. C. and Mellbin, T. 1979. "Obesity in 10 year olds: an epidemiological study", *Pediatrics*, 64(5), pp. 564–572

Ware, H. 1973. "The limits of acceptable family size: evidence from Melbourne, Australia", *Journal Biosocial Science*, 5, pp. 309 328

Watford, R. H. 1976. *A Study of Attitudes of Elementary Teachers towards Only Children*, Unpublished Doctoral dissertation, University of North Carolina (Quoted in Hawke and Knox 1977)

Watson, P. J. and Biderman, M. D. 1989. "Failure of only-child status to predict narcissism", *Perceptual and Motor Skills*, 69, p. 1346

Weiss, R. S. 1979. *Going it Alone*, New York: Basic Books

Wenger, G. C. 1984. *The Supportive Network – Coping with Old Age*, Allen and Unwin

Werner, B. and Chalk, S. 1986. "Projections of first, second, third and later births", *Population Trends*, 46, pp. 26–34

Wilson, K. and Knox, D. 1981. "Occupational commitments of mothers in one child families", *Free Inquiry in Creative Sociology*, 9(2), pp. 162–165

Zajonc, R. B. and Marcus, G. B. 1975. "Birth order and intellectual development", *Psychological Review*, 82, pp. 74–88

NCDS Secondary Analysis Results

The results presented here are based on secondary analysis of data from the National Child Development Study. The results are presented in the order in which they are described in the text.

Background of only children and one-sibling children (all families)

	Only ch.	1-sib ch.
Occupation of mother's husband: middle class	31%	37%
skilled working class	57%	49%
unskilled	12%	14%
Father figure left school at 14/15	61%	54%
Mother figure left school at 14/15	51%	41%
Mother working full or part time when child was 7	42%	28%
Family had sole use of amenities when child was 7	79%	86%
Mean age of mother at birth of child (yrs)	28.5	26.9
No father figure when child was 16	8%	5%
Boys	44%	52%
Girls	56%	48%

Outcomes for only and one-sibling children (two-parent families only)
(On the majority of items examined, no statistically significant difference was found between only children and children with one sibling; these results are listed as "NS". On items where a statistically significant difference in outcome emerged, percentages or means have been given; all such differences were confirmed as significant when background factors were allowed for. Complete results will be published elsewhere.)

	Only ch.		1-sib ch.
Mean score on Maths/Arithmetic Test at 7	-	NS	-
at 11	-	NS	-
at 16	-	NS	-
Mean score on Reading/Comprehension Test at 7	-	NS	-
at 11	18.95		18.16
at 16	-	NS	-
Mean score on General Ability Test at 11	-	NS	-
Awareness of world at 7	-	NS	-
Creativity at 7	-	NS	-
General knowledge at 11	-	NS	-
Child outstanding in any respect at 11	-	NS	-
Aspirations (exams, further education, jobs) at 16	-	NS	-
Employment status at 23	-	NS	-

	Only ch.		1-sib ch.
Social position of current/last job at 23	-	NS	-
Mean score on measure of Home Behaviour at 7	-	NS	-
at 11	-	NS	-
at 16	-	NS	-
Mean score on measure of School Behaviour at 7	-	NS	-
at 11	-	NS	-
at 16	-	NS	-
Mean score on Malaise Inventory at 23	-	NS	-
Seen by psychiatrist/psychologist at 7	-	NS	-
at 11	-	NS	-
at 16	-	NS	-
at 23	1%		3%
Psychiatric/emotional problems between 16 and 23	1%		4%
Mean score on measure of Academic Motivation at 16 (lower score denotes higher motivation)	17.21		18.33
Children frequently engaged in indoor activities at 11	39%		33%
Children frequently engaged in outdoor activities at 11	33%		43%
Sometimes/often bored at 11	66%		75%
Enjoyed spare time at 11	34%		25%
Children meeting friends out of school most days at 7	-	NS	-
at 11	-	NS	-
Frequency of attending parties, dancing, discos at 16	-	NS	
at 23	-	NS	-
Frequency of visiting friends and kin at 23	-	NS	-
Average weekly pocket money at 16	£4.88		£4.38
Read to at least once a week by mother at 7	67%		57%
Read to at least once a week by father at 7	55%		43%
Frequency of helping about the house at 11	-	NS	-
Parents with strong views on child's appearance at 16	-	NS	-
Parents asked where child went in the evenings at 16	-	NS	-
Parents disapproved of child's friends at 16	-	NS	-
Parents overconcerned about child's education at 7	-	NS	-
at 11	-	NS	-
at 16	-	NS	-
Parents very anxious for child to do well at 16	-	NS	-
Overdependent on mother at 7	29%		21%
Got on well with mother and father at 16	-	NS	-
Mean score on measure of pt/ch agreement at 16	22.44		21.97
Still living at home at 23	-	NS	-
Overweight at 7	-	NS	-
at 11	18%		9%
at 16	12%		8%
at 23	-	NS	-

Index

HMSO publications are available from:

HMSO Bookshops
71 Lothian Road, Edinburgh, EH3 9AZ
031-228 4181 Fax 031-229 2734
49 High Holborn, London, WC1V 6HB
071-873 0011 Fax 071-873 8200 (counter service only)
258 Broad Street, Birmingham, B1 2HE
021-643 3740 Fax 021-643 6510
33 Wine Street, Bristol, BS1 2BQ
0272 264306 Fax 0272 294515
9-21 Princess Street, Manchester, M60 8AS
061-834 7201 Fax 061-833 0634
16 Arthur Street, Belfast, BT1 4GD
0232 238451 Fax 0232 235401

HMSO Publications Centre
(Mail, fax and telephone orders only)
PO Box 276, London, SW8 5DT
Telephone orders 071-873 9090
General enquiries 071-873 0011
(queuing system in operation for both numbers)
Fax orders 071-873 8200

HMSO's Accredited Agents
(see Yellow Pages)
and through good booksellers

Printed in Scotland for HMSO by CC No 13129 35C 9/94